LEO
2004

Jane Struthers

p

This is a Parragon Book
First published in 2003

Parragon
Queen Street House
4 Queen Street
Bath BA1 1HE
UK

Produced by Magpie Books, an imprint of
Constable & Robinson Ltd, London

Illustrations courtesy of Slatter-Anderson, London
Cover courtesy of Simon Levy

ISBN 1-40541-565-7

A copy of the British Library Cataloguing-in-Publication Data
is available from the British Library

Printed and bound in the EU

CONTENTS

Introduction 1

Chapter One
The Year 2004 3

Chapter Two
Your Leo Sun Sign 109

Chapter Three
Love and the Stars 115

Chapter Four
Your Astrological Holiday Guide 140

Chapter Five
Born on the Cusp? 148

Dates for 2004

Leo 23 July – 23 August

Virgo 24 August – 23 September

Libra 24 September – 23 October

Scorpio 24 October – 22 November

Sagittarius 23 November – 21 December

Capricorn 22 December – 20 January

Aquarius 21 January – 18 February

Pisces 19 February – 20 March

Aries 21 March – 20 April

Taurus 21 April – 21 May

Gemini 22 May – 21 June

Cancer 22 June – 22 July

INTRODUCTION

Dear Leo

Happy New Year! I hope that 2004 is everything you want it to be, and more. If you're a clever Leo you'll want to make the very best of the opportunities coming your way in the year ahead, which is why this book is so useful. It will help you to maximize your many chances and show you how to deal with any problem areas that you encounter.

My summary of 2004 in **The Year 2004** tells you exactly what you can expect in your relationships, health, money and career this year, and how to make the most of them. This is followed by my day-by-day forecasts for 2004, complete with at-a-glance charts that show you the general trend for each month.

Being born under the sign of Leo gives you a special set of characteristics, and you can read all about them in **Your Leo Sun Sign**. It's divided into four sections describing your relationships, health, money and career, so you can get a thorough insight into your personality. If some of your relationships have been puzzling you recently, you need to read **Love and the Stars** to discover what's going on. It describes your compatibility with each of the twelve signs, and is followed by two charts that show how you get on with the other signs in love and sex, and also as friends.

Everyone needs to get away from it all every now and then, and holidays can be good for our health. If you've ever wondered which is the ideal holiday for your Leo Sun sign, turn to **Your Astrological Holiday Guide** to discover which destinations and activities will suit you best.

If you were born at the beginning or end of Leo you may have always wondered if you're really a Leo or whether you're a Cancerian or a Virgo instead. Well, you can finally solve the mystery by turning to **Born on the Cusp?** and discovering which is your true Sun sign.

This book is all you need to get the very best out of 2004, so have fun and make it a great year!

Jane Struthers

THE YEAR 2004

Friends and Lovers

Love makes your world go round but it could also make it seem a bit bumpy in 2004, thanks to the antics of certain people. They may be absolutely determined to get their own way, apparently at whatever cost is necessary, or perhaps you behave like this with them. There's also a chance that you could become embroiled in a compulsive relationship that grips you like a vice, especially if you were born between 11 and 16 August. If this happens you will have to struggle to retain your objectivity, but do your best – otherwise you could be overwhelmed by the impact this person has on you.

You may also be very idealistic about some of the people in your life this year, refusing to believe anything but the very best about them. Although you're too big-hearted to entertain suspicions about anyone for long, you should try not to be so trusting that you enable people to run rings around you or double-cross you. On the other hand, there's a chance that you'll be swept off your feet by a Prince or Princess Charming who turns your life into the last chapter of a fairy story in which everyone lives happily ever after. Aah!

If you're currently a single Leo who's looking for a partner, between September and the end of the year your best bet is to search for them in local situations and at neighbourhood events. Even if you don't meet the man or woman of your dreams, you could make some very good friends who'll give you plenty of laughs.

Health

You aren't usually prone to worry but certain anxieties will nag away at you this year if you let them. It could be difficult to put your finger on what's wrong, and you may even be reluctant to do so because that would mean facing up to some unpleasant truths that you'd rather shove to the back of your mind for the time being. However, you would be wise to look your fears in the face because otherwise they'll prey on your mind and possibly even undermine your health by interfering with your sleep or draining your energy.

It's important that you get plenty of fresh air and exercise in 2004, especially from late September onwards. You'll relish the prospect of getting out into the open whenever you have the chance, and short changes of scene will also do you good. For instance, you might decide to arrange several weekends away to keep you going until your next holiday.

Pay extra attention to your health between July and August, and again in January and December. These are all periods when the more effort you put into staying fit and healthy, the greater the results will be. If you suspect that you'd benefit from changing your diet or going on a short detox, try to do it in November when your body will respond very well to any improvements you want to make.

Money

No self-respecting Leo can be without money because there are so many things that you need to spend it on. So it's good news this year that your finances look very healthy, especially between January and late September. If you're lucky you could receive a small windfall or there might be an increase in your earning power. This is also a very good period for doing some wheeling and dealing and if you're clever you'll end up making a healthy profit, although you might not pocket millions. However, be careful with your outgoings, or all the money that flows in your direction will quickly flow away again in an orgy of spending and gracious living. So mind how you go!

Another reason why you'd be wise to be careful with your cash is that some of your financial arrangements could go slightly haywire. If you share your resources with your partner, one of you may have to rely on the other more than usual, or there could be an unexpected increase in your general expenses. Keep an eagle eye on credit card statements, mortgage payments, tax bills and anything else that involves official money matters, just in case things turn go awry for no apparent reason. Mind you, there's also a chance that you could end the year much better off than when you started it, all because some surprise money comes your way. For instance, you could get a tax rebate out of the blue or receive a financial gift when you were least expecting it. So be prepared for all financial eventualities in 2004!

Career

You're usually a very sociable creature but in 2004 you'll be happiest if you can be left to your own devices for long stretches of time. This means that you'll get on best in your career if you can be allowed to work by yourself. So this might be the year in which you decide to become self-employed or opt to work from home instead of at the office. Alternatively, your boss might give you a project that keeps you apart from your workmates. Although you'll enjoy working on your own, try to resist the temptation to work around the clock, particularly if you're worried that you aren't doing a good enough job. Such a strategy will only wear you out and mean that you can't do your best because your energy is so depleted.

From late September onwards, you'll make progress in any activities that involve communicating with others. For instance, you might go on lots of short journeys in the course of your job or have to learn how to use a computer if you can't already do so. Any job that's connected with buying and selling, transport, magazines or newspapers, cars or telephones will go well for you and might also involve some lucky breaks.

Your Day by Day Guide

JANUARY AT A GLANCE

Love	♥ ♥ ♥ ♥ ♥
Money	£ $
Career	💻 💻 💻 💻 💻
Health	☼ ☼ ☼ ☼ ☼

• *Thursday 1 January* •

Happy New Year! You're filled with conviction and determination today, so write down your New Year resolutions if you haven't already done so. Today is also a good opportunity to fill in all the relevant details in your new diary, so you don't lose any valuable information. This will be a helpful distraction if you become impatient with anyone who isn't doing things in the way you'd like. You might also lose your temper about some travel arrangements, but try to stay calm if possible.

• *Friday 2 January* •

You're efficient and businesslike today, which is just what you need if you're back at work after the holidays. You'll quite enjoy getting back into your usual routine, and the happy atmosphere with colleagues will help. If you've decided that this is the year in which you change jobs or apply for promotion, start planning your strategy. There's no time like the present!

• *Saturday 3 January* •

Loved ones need careful handling today, and even then they're likely to behave in ways you weren't expecting. For instance, a partner might announce that they need some time to themselves when you were looking forward to being together. You might also be brought up short about a joint or official money matter, and feel that the rug's been pulled out from under you.

• *Sunday 4 January* •

Life is treating you in a kinder fashion today, and you're feeling much more cheerful and calm. This is a super day for being with people who are dear to your heart, whether they're friends or family. If you haven't seen some people recently you might be inspired to give them a ring or invite them round for a drink.

• *Monday 5 January* •

A friend opens doors for you or inspires you about something today, and you'll feel better as a result. This is also a good day for making progress in some travel arrangements, especially if that means reaching decisions or putting your money where your mouth is. If you've been wondering whether to continue your education in some way, you'll now know what to do next.

• *Tuesday 6 January* •

An in-depth conversation reveals a new side to a certain person today. They might let you into a secret or let their hair down in some way, so you feel you're getting to know them even better than ever. If you've got a crush on someone and are hoping that no one has noticed, be careful not to reveal too much now, especially when you're caught unawares.

• *Wednesday 7 January* •

Today's Full Moon is urging you to face up to certain unpleasant facts and to stare them in the face during the coming fortnight. This is the only way to resolve them, even if it does take courage. Besides, you're reaching the point where you know you've got to do something constructive and it will certainly be a relief not to have to worry about all this any longer. So take action!

• *Thursday 8 January* •

This is a day for going over projects and ventures that have already got off the ground, and making sure that everything is progressing nicely. Unfortunately, however, you won't get anywhere if you start anything new now. It might soon grind to a halt, or you could discover that you've made some errors so that you have to start again from scratch.

• *Friday 9 January* •

Your employment prospects look excellent today, so bear that in mind if you're currently on the hunt for a new job because you could strike lucky. On the other hand, a fantastic opportunity might apparently land in your lap without you having to lift a finger. If this happens it will be thanks to all the hard work you've done in the past, and also thanks to the good reputation that you've built up as a result.

• *Saturday 10 January* •

Relationships are a little fraught today because someone is setting too much store by them. You might have to pay a lot of attention to a partner who's feeling neglected, or you could have to mediate between two people who are competing with each other in some way. This is nothing to worry about and it will soon blow over, but it will keep your diplomacy skills busy in the meantime.

• *Sunday 11 January* •

Financial matters lead to surprises today, so be prepared. You might discover that there's a discrepancy in your bank or credit card account, or you could find that your other half has made some surprise financial moves. Watch out if you're near the shops or browsing a favourite web site because impulse buys look very likely but you may not like the items once you've got them home.

• *Monday 12 January* •

You'll really enjoy your daily routine this Monday and everything will go well. You could also win the co-operation of workmates and customers, helping to make life easy for you. You might decide to buy something that improves your health or boosts your fitness level, whether it's a bottle of vitamin pills or the membership of a gym.

• *Tuesday 13 January* •

It's highly likely that you'll fall out with a loved one over money today. Maybe you don't approve of what they're spending their money on, or they think you're being too extravagant. Try not to let the situation get out of hand, so that you end up having a right old set-to about something that doesn't really merit so much fuss. Maybe the row is really about something quite different?

• *Wednesday 14 January* •

Between now and early February is a very auspicious time for using your brain in the course of your job. You might be asked to take part in a think tank or to get involved in some negotiations, or you may have to work your way through a pile of paperwork. Your day-to-day life will be busier than usual, making it important to keep track of all your commitments and chores.

• *Thursday 15 January* •

Someone's being a bit critical today. You might even accuse them of being pedantic, especially if they're fussing over things that you don't think are important. Or maybe it's the other way round and you're the one who's dotting every I and crossing every T as though your life depended on it. Either way, try to keep everything in proportion and don't get your knickers in a twist.

• *Friday 16 January* •

You're viewing the world through rose-tinted glasses today, although you won't realize it at the time. You might wallow in a haze of nostalgia, convincing yourself that things were so much better in the past or rewriting history where a certain person is concerned. Try not to let this land you in trouble by making you gullible and allowing others to take advantage of you.

• *Saturday 17 January* •

This is a terrific day for keeping up with all the chores and mundane tasks that are on the agenda, whether that means doing some DIY, going shopping or cleaning the house. What's more, all this will be surprisingly enjoyable and satisfying, because you'll want to do as good a job as possible. If you're entertaining a workmate at home, you'll have a great time.

• *Sunday 18 January* •

You're in an expansive and extravagant mood today. You'll grab any chance to spend money, whether you're in a favourite shop or standing a round of drinks in the pub, which won't be very good news if you're supposed to be saving up at the moment. Your heartfelt feelings for a certain person will spill out, too, whether you want them to or not.

• *Monday 19 January* •

Introduce some adventure into your day, or you'll start to feel fed up and restless. You're on the hunt for excitement and stimulation, and you'll make a beeline for anyone who can offer them. This means you could be attracted to someone who's supposed to be off limits, or you might dare to take some risks purely in order to get your adrenalin going. Be careful!

• *Tuesday 20 January* •

This is a terrific day for making changes in your life, especially if you're prepared to do something that seems quite drastic or extreme. You've got plenty of will-power right now but you should be careful how you use it. You won't get very far if you try to introduce changes that will benefit you but inconvenience everyone else. So make sure your motives are honourable.

• *Wednesday 21 January* •

Team work is the way forward during the next two weeks. You'll feel happiest when working in tandem with others and you'll gain a lot from their company. If you're about to make an emotional commitment to someone you couldn't have chosen a better time, and your relationship will blossom in many wonderful ways.

• *Thursday 22 January* •

Go carefully because this looks like being a tricky day. For a start, there's a lot of criticism flying about, whether you're finding fault with yourself or someone else is doing it for you. Some of this criticism may be justified but a lot of it is probably unfair and over the top. Don't allow it to put you off your stroke because, with a little concentration, you can make tremendous progress now. Have faith in yourself and in your abilities.

• *Friday 23 January* •

This is a super day to spend with partners and some of your favourite people. There's a very strong rapport between you right now, bringing out the best in one another. If the atmosphere has been slightly fraught with a certain person recently, today is a great opportunity to talk about what went wrong between you and then to work hard at getting things back on track.

• *Saturday 24 January* •

How important is a certain person to you? It's a good question to ponder today, particularly if there have been problems between you lately or you aren't entirely sure about the role they play in your life. Be prepared to look into your heart in order to find the answers, and also to be honest with yourself about this. You may as well not bother if you're going to fool yourself.

• *Sunday 25 January* •

The atmosphere between you and a certain person could either get very heated or very chilly today, and either way it won't be comfortable. That's because one, if not both, of you is taking things too much to heart and is quite likely to make a meal of the smallest problem. If one of you is feeling jealous or resentful about something, it will soon become a cause for conflict. Take care!

• *Monday 26 January* •

Life starts to return to normal after yesterday's difficulties, much to your relief. Do your utmost to ensure that this happens, especially if you've got to eat humble pie and admit that you were in the wrong. If you can do this with love and humour, it won't be nearly such a big deal. Social events are really enjoyable today, and might even have romantic overtones.

• *Tuesday 27 January* •

Try not to let yourself get bogged down in duty or the mundane side of life, because that will soon make you feel ratty and fed up. Instead, try to rise above such niggles, and tackle the chores with a glad heart. Unfortunately, this might be easier said than done, thanks to the nit-picking attitude of you-know-who, but it's by no means impossible. So keep smiling!

• *Wednesday 28 January* •

You're in a risk-taking mood today, and the last thing you want to do is to play safe. That's all very well in moderation, but don't do anything foolish as it will backfire on you. Be especially careful if you're driving because you might be tempted to go over the speed limit or be more reckless than usual. A travel plan sets you a challenge, but you're more than ready to meet it.

• *Thursday 29 January* •

Is it your imagination or is someone being rather bossy? They may think that they know what's best for you, but you beg to differ. You may have to be tactful about how you handle this, because it would be very easy to let the situation deteriorate into a battle of wills or a furious argument. This won't be good news if you fall out with someone who's in a position of authority over you.

• *Friday 30 January* •

If you went overboard yesterday and lost your temper, this is your chance to make amends. Once you've got that out of the way, you can enjoy what promises to be a very harmonious day. What's more, someone might show their appreciation of your recent hard work by giving you a tip or perk, or they may simply pay you a nice compliment.

• *Saturday 31 January* •

Everyone is being very co-operative and helpful today, whether it's expected of them or they're doing it out of the goodness of their heart. You'll want to return the favour, making it a very happy Saturday. If you want to turn a colleague into a lover, get chatting to them or invite them out for a drink. They may not immediately fall into your arms but you'll get a good idea of whether you're wasting your time.

FEBRUARY AT A GLANCE

Love	♥ ♥ ♥ ♥ ♥
Money	£ $ £ $ £
Career	💻 💻 💻 💻
Health	☼ ☼ ☼

• *Sunday 1 February* •

It's another of those days when you need to tread with dainty feet when dealing with loved ones. Something has got into them, making them unreasonable, heated and liable to turn a minor snag into a major drama in two seconds flat. Or so you think, although they may try to pin the blame on you! Rather than get involved in an endless round of recriminations, it will be much more productive to find out what's wrong and then do something about it.

• *Monday 2 February* •

Relationships could either bring you spiritual satisfaction or total confusion today. It all depends on how grounded and realistic you're feeling. It's essential that you don't fall into the trap of kidding yourself about someone's motives or turning a blind eye to their obvious faults. If you can manage to avoid this you could have a very moving and powerful encounter with someone, possibly even giving you hints about why you're together.

• *Tuesday 3 February* •

During the next six weeks you'll be fired with enthusiasm and determination, especially when it comes to making a name for yourself or getting ahead in your career. You'll experience a sense of urgency about all this but don't turn that into an excuse to use anyone as a stepping stone to the top, or to get what you want from them and then discard them like an old handkerchief. If you do anything like this you can bet that it will rebound on you sooner or later.

• *Wednesday 4 February* •

This is a terrific day for nestling close to a certain person and enjoying their company. This might be a close chum or it could be your one true love, but you won't really care as long as you get some emotional satisfaction from the encounter. If you're with someone who always makes your heart beat faster, things could get very erotic and romantic in no time at all.

• *Thursday 5 February* •

This is a day for showing your mettle and proving that you've got what it takes to put yourself on the map. You probably won't achieve your ultimate aim today but nevertheless your confidence in yourself will grow, and certain people will be watching your progress with great interest. If you've got to issue orders, do so with grace and diplomacy.

• *Friday 6 February* •

Today's Full Moon is the trigger for you to clear your life of anything that has outlived its usefulness. This might be a cupboard full of clutter that you no longer need or it could be certain habits that are holding you back from achieving your best. So start clearing the decks during the next two weeks and notice the difference this makes.

• *Saturday 7 February* •

The best way to get on well with partners and friends during the next three weeks will be to talk to them about whatever seems important at the time. So don't keep your thoughts to yourself because it will be much more productive to discuss them with someone. This will also be a good time to take part in a negotiation or some form of mediation.

• *Sunday 8 February* •

You'll have the opportunity to branch out in new directions between now and early March, especially if this involves travel of the mind, body or soul. For instance, if you're about to jet off on holiday then you'll have a whale of a time, and it will have a big impact on you. There's also a chance that you'll lose your heart to an idea, a belief, a cause or a person from a different walk of life from yours.

• *Monday 9 February* •

Someone is being altogether too hasty and irascible today, making it difficult to be around them for long without getting the sharp end of their tongue. Unfortunately, you may also be behaving like this, especially if you're feeling stymied or trapped by circumstances beyond your control. For instance, you might be chafing under the yoke of current responsibilities, yet know that you've got to grit your teeth and just get on with them.

• *Tuesday 10 February* •

Yesterday's grouchy mood has vanished, leaving you with a very sunny and peaceful disposition. It's a lovely day for simply enjoying the company of whoever happens to be around and you'll find something about them to like, even if they aren't usually your favourite person. All the same, take care not to give them the wrong impression about your feelings for them, especially if you suspect that they have a soft spot for you.

• *Wednesday 11 February* •

If a relationship has left something to be desired recently, today is a marvellous opportunity to work together to introduce some positive changes. Be prepared to talk about your side of the story and to listen to the other person too, because then you'll really make some headway. This is also a terrific day to put your head together with someone and dream up some creative ideas.

• *Thursday 12 February* •

The better you know someone, the more likely it is that you'll fall out with them today. This spat won't last long but it won't be very pleasant while it does, and you might find that you've said things in the heat of the moment that you'd never have said if you were feeling more calm. Better undo the damage as soon as possible, so that no one has a chance to resent what's happened.

• *Friday 13 February* •

It's another day when tempers are frayed and people are likely to go off bang about the smallest little thing. Once again, it's the people who you're closest to who are likely to inflame you the most, especially if you're fuming inside about something that they've done. Get it off your chest, but don't make a song and dance about it if it isn't really that important.

• *Saturday 14 February* •

There's a rather miserable atmosphere around you today, making you feel slightly disconnected from everyone else.

There may be a good reason for this, perhaps because you're physically separated from loved ones. Alternatively, you might be conscious of an emotional gap between you that can't be breached right now. Is it a temporary blip or something more serious?

• *Sunday 15 February* •

It's very difficult to keep your thoughts straight today and they're highly likely to mislead you in some way. You might get the wrong end of the stick with a partner and imagine that they're saying one thing when they're actually telling you something very different. Try to be straightforward yourself, to reduce the chance of getting your wires crossed.

• *Monday 16 February* •

Quite frankly, you're probably better off being left to your own devices today. That's because you're in a very self-contained mood and you're also feeling rather fed up. Although you might want other people to cheer you up, they're more likely to increase your sense of wretchedness in some way. Channel your energies into your work so you can achieve something.

• *Tuesday 17 February* •

Hard work brings its own rewards today. You might get a big pat on the back from someone who's impressed with what you've done, and you'll also have the satisfaction of knowing that you've done a good job. There could be news about a bonus or perk that's coming your way, and if you know you're due for a pay rise you'll have fun working out how you're going to spend it.

• *Wednesday 18 February* •

Don't be in too much of a hurry to get things done today – it will be a recipe for hassle and bad temper. You'll soon wind yourself up into a spin, so you don't know what to do first and end up going round in circles. There's also the chance that you'll become clumsy or careless, and have to do something twice because you made a hash of it first time round. So slow down!

• *Thursday 19 February* •

During the coming four weeks you'll want to concentrate on close and intimate partnerships more than usual, especially if this means getting down to analysing why these people are in your life. Now, this will be a waste of time if you want to gloss over your feelings or desires, so you must be prepared to look at what's going on in a lot of detail, whether you think it's good or bad.

• *Friday 20 February* •

Any form of discussion or meeting will go really well today, helped by your ability to say what you think. Of course, there are days when saying what you think is guaranteed to cause problems, but today everyone is very receptive to your ideas and they're willing to hear you out. Make sure you repay the compliment and all will be well.

• *Saturday 21 February* •

Your emotions exert a lot of power over you today, and at times you may feel that you're held in their grip. Do your best to ensure that this doesn't create difficulties. You'll inject a lot of energy and drive into your close relationships, and also in your dealings with people who have power or authority over you.

• *Sunday 22 February* •

There could be a surprise connected with your joint or official money matters today, perhaps when a partner gives you some startling news. Alternatively, a close relationship will give you pause for thought, making you reassess it in the light of what happens now. For example, you may realize that you need more emotional freedom than you're getting at the moment or that you're disappointed in a partner.

• *Monday 23 February* •

You're intrigued by the world today and want to explore it in some way. Whatever you choose to do, you'll enjoy it most if it engages your emotions on some level. You could be attracted to a different religion or belief from your own, or feel a passionate conviction about an idea or philosophy. There could also be a deliciously warm exchange with a friend who lives abroad.

• *Tuesday 24 February* •

It's very difficult to assess a certain person's motives today, possibly because you don't want to think badly of them even though all the evidence against them looks pretty dire. Unfortunately, your thinking isn't nearly as clear-cut as you might imagine right now, so avoid jumping to conclusions or confusing your hunches with solid facts. Wait and see what happens before making any decisions about what to do next.

• *Wednesday 25 February* •

It's an excellent day for planning your next financial move, whether you're simply deciding when you can afford to pay some bills or you're going to be switching large chunks of money from one investment to another. You'll prefer to do all this in private, and if you do take anyone into your confidence you'll have to trust them implicitly.

• *Thursday 26 February* •

You've got a tremendous amount of confidence today, so it's great for pushing ahead at work. As a result, a long-term plan might get closer to fruition or you could make a big impression on someone who'll be very influential in the future. You're in a slightly daredevil mood, so be careful if that makes you want to splash money in all directions. Can you afford it?

• *Friday 27 February* •

Something happens in a special relationship today, bringing you closer together in all sorts of ways. If you've been hoping that you-know-who would finally recognize your existence and smother you with burning kisses, that might happen now. It's certainly a day in which love could change your life in some way, so be prepared for some overwhelming events!

• *Saturday 28 February* •

Is someone feeling jealous or possessive? It certainly seems that way, judging by their behaviour at the moment. They might resent the amount of time you're going to spend with a friend, or possibly even accuse you of infidelity. There could also be a dust-up with a chum over money or possessions. Not an easy day, but don't make things more difficult by over-reacting.

• *Sunday 29 February* •

You're in a very grounded and realistic frame of mind today, giving you a good perspective on everything that's going on in your life at the moment. You'll have a better idea of whether something is really a crisis or whether it's a minor inconvenience that will soon melt away. You might also reach an important decision about a financial or emotional matter.

MARCH AT A GLANCE

Love	♥ ♥ ♥ ♥
Money	£ $ £ $ £
Career	💻 💻 💻
Health	☼ ☼

• *Monday 1 March* •

This is another day when your emotions are flowing well, making you receptive to people and able to bring out the best in them. Ideally, you should get together with some of the special people in your life and forget about the rest of the world. If you're in the mood for romance, set the scene and then let nature take its course.

• *Tuesday 2 March* •

You're capable of a lot of hard work but you'll make the most progress if you can get on without any interruptions from others. As a result, you may prefer to lock yourself away somewhere and not come out until you've finished. Don't worry if you've got one eye on the clock because you'll manage to get everything done in time, provided you organize your time efficiently and don't get into a panic.

• *Wednesday 3 March* •

Try to take things in your stride today. Otherwise they're likely to take on too much significance and get you in a bit of a state. There's a strong chance that you could get upset about something that is supposed to be a secret but which finally sees the light of day now because you can't help mentioning it. You could also be disturbed by something that clashes with one of your beliefs.

• *Thursday 4 March* •

It's easy to get carried away today and to say or do too much, so watch out. Your greatest stumbling block is likely to be your finances, giving you a tendency to overspend or to boast of something that you own or are about to buy. Be careful about this because it could leave you out of pocket or give the impression that you're much more materialistic than you really are.

• *Friday 5 March* •

During the rest of the month you'd do well to butter up anyone who could help you to get ahead in your career. Now, this doesn't mean being insincere and sucking up to them, only to reject them the moment you've got what you want from them. Instead, you must be fair and not give the wrong impression, nor promise things that you can't or won't deliver when the chips are down.

• *Saturday 6 March* •

If your finances have got you into a pretty pickle lately, today's Full Moon gives you the chance to extract yourself from the mess during the coming fortnight. You might have to set yourself a strict budget, provided you know you can stick to it, or have to pay off some debts. You may also have to readjust your attitude towards your finances in order to avoid trouble in future.

• *Sunday 7 March* •

If you did some serious thinking about your money matters yesterday you'll already have some pretty good ideas about what to do for the best. Well, strike while the iron's hot even if you can't do as much as you'd like immediately. Write down your ideas, talk to people who might be able to help, or pick the brains of someone whose wisdom you respect.

• *Monday 8 March* •

This is another brilliant day for making progress in any financial matters that are currently bugging you. You're determined to get answers to your questions, and this will be much easier than you might have imagined. For instance, someone in a position of power could be very helpful or they might suggest the very solution you've been considering.

• *Tuesday 9 March* •

You could be dazzled by the attractions of a certain person today, especially if you meet them for work or financial reasons. One look at them and you'll be hooked. However, the chemistry between you may not last, although it will be very exciting while it does. You could also receive a surprising proposition from the last person you would have expected to suggest such a thing.

• *Wednesday 10 March* •

It's very easy for a certain someone to get in a stew today, taking everything much more seriously than usual and causing a fuss as a result. Be prepared to soothe their fevered brow, even if you do think they're over-reacting. Mind you, the boot could be on the other foot if you start to feel competitive or are worried that you-know-who is going to steal a march on you.

• *Thursday 11 March* •

This is a marvellous day for getting out your calculator and sorting out your domestic financial arrangements, particularly if you're trying to make ends meet at the moment or you've got to work out a budget for a forthcoming project. You'll have an eye for a bargain if you're doing some household shopping, and will be pleased with the money-saving deals you spot.

• *Friday 12 March* •

If you aren't careful there will be a hothouse atmosphere with a loved one, with both of you becoming more heated and annoyed by the hour. In these conditions, what starts out as a vague niggle with one another will quickly grow into a searing row in which buried resentments are exhumed and recriminations fly about like feathers. Keep a strong grip on your emotions!

• *Saturday 13 March* •

Once again the emotional temperature is higher than you'd like and there's every chance that you'll fall out with loved ones. Thankfully, the atmosphere isn't as corrosive and tense as it was yesterday, so you may be able to clear the air eventually. However, try to resist the temptation to dredge up any complaints that didn't get an airing yesterday. What good will that do?

• *Sunday 14 March* •

Let's face it, you've got a lot on your plate at the moment and it's starting to get you down. In fact, you might encounter the straw that broke the camel's back today, perhaps when someone asks you if you can find the time to do them a favour or you realize that other people are having fun while you're slogging your guts out. You've had enough! So what are you going to do about it?

• *Monday 15 March* •

Life is a bit fraught right now and the tension continues today. You could easily begin to doubt yourself and your abilities, possibly even making self-deprecating comments to other people. Try not to do this, even though it's tempting, because it will plant negative thoughts about you in the minds of others, and will also make you feel wretched in the process.

• *Tuesday 16 March* •

You're a little more upbeat and positive today, especially if you're busy with your work. You'll be able to chug along nicely, and it's also a good day for weighing up the pros and cons if you've got to make a decision. Make the most of your Leonine organizational skills by getting to grips with paperwork, forms or your accounts.

• *Wednesday 17 March* •

You're in the mood to spend money today, so be careful! This extravagant streak will be especially noticeable if you're looking for work clothes or an outfit to wear at an important social event, because money will be no object once you spot the perfect thing. If you're going out on a date with someone who's trying to impress you, they'll pull out all the stops and flash their credit card in all directions.

• *Thursday 18 March* •

Roll up your sleeves and get on with whatever is top of your list of priorities. You're in a very determined and go-getting mood, making you want to cut to the chase and make as much progress as possible. Ideally, you should work in tandem with someone who can give you valuable feedback and encouragement. But don't let any hint of competitiveness come between you.

• *Friday 19 March* •

You aren't seeing someone in their true light today. Instead, you're putting a gloss on their actions and brushing certain things under the mental carpet. This may not matter if you wise up to what's happening by tomorrow, but it will cause problems if you continue to kid yourself about what's going on with this person. You need to take off those rose-tinted spectacles.

• *Saturday 20 March* •

Exciting opportunities will beckon during the coming fortnight, so make sure you're ready for them when they appear. Some of them may be disguised, so you have to investigate them thoroughly before realizing their true worth. This means you can't go solely by appearances, because something that looks promising may turn out to be hollow, and vice versa.

• *Sunday 21 March* •

Between now and early May you'll enjoy putting lots of energy into leisure-time activities. They'll be a wonderful way for you to relax and take the pressure off other areas of your life, especially if they offer you a complete change of pace. Friends will also keep you busy now, but sometimes they could make you impatient or ratty too, especially when they're too slow or timid for you.

• *Monday 22 March* •

You have a very enquiring mind today and you'll love giving it some exercise. This is a fabulous day to do some research, perhaps by browsing on the net or looking something up in your local library. If you've got the time you'll enjoy curling up with a good book, particularly if it teaches you more about a religion, spiritual belief, ethical code or environmental crusade.

• *Tuesday 23 March* •

You usually like a structure to your day but you'll do your best work right now if you can be flexible and go where the mood takes you. This means you might switch from one task to another when you get bored, or have a brainstorming session with a colleague and then spend the rest of the day alone. Don't be frightened to pursue ideas that seem slightly wacky or unconventional.

• *Wednesday 24 March* •

Speak up, because you've got some very interesting things to say today. You can also be pretty sure of having an appreciative audience, so there's little danger of your words of wisdom falling on stony ground. You'll go straight to the top of the class if you're at school or college, and you'll also emerge with flying colours if you're taking part in a discussion.

• *Thursday 25 March* •

You're in a dynamic mood and you don't want to sit around twiddling your thumbs. In fact, you'll get pretty annoyed if that's what you have to do, perhaps because someone is slowing you up or circumstances are stacked against you. Release any pent-up nervous energy by doing something physical or therapeutic.

• *Friday 26 March* •

It's important that you keep smiling today, or your mood will quickly plummet and you'll start to feel miserable. However, you need to be realistic about whatever is happening to you at the moment, or you'll be caught in a clash between foolish optimism and suffocating pessimism. It may help to put your thoughts down on paper.

• *Saturday 27 March* •

The tension between you and a loved one is mounting, and it will be stretched to breaking point if you don't do something about it. It's highly likely that you're allowing things to build up in your mind where they'll assume gigantic proportions. Once this happens, you'll feel as though you're caught in an all-or-nothing situation, even though this is far from the truth.

• *Sunday 28 March* •

Someone dear to your heart is determined to go their own way today, and it seems there's very little you can do about it. In fact, if you're wise you'll let them do their own thing because that's the quickest way for them to get it out of their system. The more you protest about their plans, the more determined they'll be to go ahead with them.

• *Monday 29 March* •

You're feeling quietly optimistic about something today, and it's done wonders for your mood. You aren't going overboard and believing all your fantasies, but neither do you think that disaster is just around the corner. Spare the time for an activity or person who always makes you feel good, or which helps to make your world go round.

• *Tuesday 30 March* •

If you want to keep certain facts a secret you'd be advised not to breathe them to a living soul today. Once you divulge them, there's a strong possibility that they'll become common knowledge, either through sheer accident or because someone can't resist spreading such juicy gossip. Confide in your diary or teddy bear, but leave it at that for the time being.

• *Wednesday 31 March* •

You end the month on a high note because you're feeling great! You've taken a very positive attitude to your current circumstances and are determined to make the best of the hand you've been dealt in the card game of life. If you're lucky, you might even find that you've got an ace up your sleeve or that your prospects for success are much greater than you dared to hope. You have everything to play for!

APRIL AT A GLANCE

Love	♥ ♥
Money	£ $
Career	💻 💻 💻 💻 💻
Health	☼ ☼

• *Thursday 1 April* •

Spend the coming six days thinking long and hard about your ambitions and goals. What do you want to achieve in 2004? Maybe you're feeling frustrated because a quarter of the year has already flown by and you have little to show for it. Well, put on your thinking cap and start devising a strategy or schedule that will inspire you to take action, so that you end the year in a much better position than when you started it. How does that sound?

• *Friday 2 April* •

Money burns a hole in your pocket today, so beware if you're supposed to be sensible with your cash at the moment. It's probably best if you keep well away from all temptation because you simply won't be able to resist it, and then you'll be annoyed with yourself later on. If you can afford to splash out, you'll be interested in luxurious or comforting items.

• *Saturday 3 April* •

From today, friends and other contacts will bring even more pleasure into your life than usual, and this happy state of affairs will last until early August. This is a marvellous chance to get to know someone better or to turn an acquaintance into a chum. There's even the possibility that what starts out as a friendship could develop into a romance during the next few weeks.

• *Sunday 4 April* •

Activities with a spiritual or religious slant will give you a lot of satisfaction today. That might mean going to a church service, visiting a sacred site or doing some meditation. Right now you're feeling connected to the world around you, rather than feeling separate from it, and you'll enjoy doing anything that enhances this experience.

• *Monday 5 April* •

You may think that you've got all the answers about a current situation or difficulty, but it seems that you'll have to re-evaluate your position during the coming fortnight. So beware of nailing your colours too firmly to the mast in case you have an embarrassing change of heart. You may also have to make a decision about a child's education, which will call for careful thought.

• *Tuesday 6 April* •

Ideally, you should avoid signing on any dotted lines between now and the 13th, in case you're making a blunder. That's because you might not be aware of all the ramifications of whatever you're agreeing to, or there could be a mistake in whatever it is you're signing. A friend is full of enthusiasm about something now and does their best to make you join in. But should you?

• *Wednesday 7 April* •

It's difficult to keep a clear head today. You're easily distracted, especially by thoughts of the past or regrets over what you should or shouldn't have done. What's more, you're showing a tendency to believe what you want to believe rather than dealing with the facts. Try to be straightforward when talking to loved ones to avoid confusing or misleading them in some way.

• *Thursday 8 April* •

It seems that a friend needs as much attention as you can give them today, and they'll be rather put out if they don't get it. So you may have to put other arrangements on hold in order to spare them the time they're demanding. You'll do all this out of the goodness of your heart and because you want to avoid a fuss, but beware of setting a precedent that you won't be able to keep.

• *Friday 9 April* •

Life has so much to offer today that you won't know where to start. The more positive your attitude, the happier and more productive the day will be. If you haven't yet planned your next holiday, today is a great chance to start thinking about where you'd like to go. And if you're taking off on a long weekend, you're all set for a wonderful time.

• *Saturday 10 April* •

Your feelings for a certain person go very deep today, stirring up all sorts of emotions that usually lie dormant inside you. Keeping such feelings to yourself will be almost impossible and it's highly likely that you'll have to express them at some point. However, try to avoid being too emotionally demanding or making this person feel obliged to respond in kind.

• *Sunday 11 April* •

You're in a very creative and expansive mood, particularly if you want to make some positive changes to your life. Right now, you have the foresight and energy to transform your world in some way, and you'll have a deep conviction that you're doing the right thing. The involvement of a certain someone in your plans will only add to your pleasure.

• *Monday 12 April* •

Things have been going really well during the past few days but you hit a snag today. It seems that there's a clash between duty and pleasure, or between freedom and responsibility. Although you'd love to do your own thing rather than what's expected of you, this will probably set you on a collision course with trouble. But, if you've got to make a stand, today is definitely the day to do it.

• *Tuesday 13 April* •

Friends and partners are terrific company today, and they'll also give you their support if it's needed. You're full of hope about a certain someone and you're pretty confident that everything is going your way. However, make sure that you're dealing with the facts rather than just indulging in wishful thinking, or you could be heading for a big disappointment.

• *Wednesday 14 April* •

Everyone's being very co-operative and helpful today, much to your delight. This is a super day for working in tandem with others, even if it's only a temporary arrangement. If you can spare the time, it's a good idea to make contact with people who you haven't seen recently. You might be inspired to arrange a reunion with them in the near future.

• *Thursday 15 April* •

Is it your imagination or is a loved one being very demanding at the moment? It certainly seems that way today, and they'll be very miffed if they can't get your attention. If you can't see them because you'll be busy with someone else, you might even get the distinct whiff of jealousy or possessiveness, which will make you feel uncomfortable. Try to play it down as much as possible.

• *Friday 16 April* •

The atmosphere between you and you-know-who is still rather tense and it shows every sign of becoming increasingly fraught today. In fact, it's highly likely that matters will come to a head between you. This is probably just as well, provided you concentrate on the main bone of contention and don't get distracted by complaints that have nothing to do with what's really going on.

• *Saturday 17 April* •

If you're feeling exhausted from the emotional problems of the past couple of days, find an escape route today. This might be through the pages of a gripping book or through a fascinating TV programme, or you might decide that the only option is a complete change of scene. A conversation will teach you something new about the world and also about yourself.

• *Sunday 18 April* •

Friends who live far away are in your thoughts today, so how about making contact with them? Ring them up, write them a chatty letter or send them an e-mail. You might even toy with the idea of arranging to visit them in the near future, or inviting them to come and stay with you. It's important that you have something to look forward to now, so make some exciting plans.

• *Monday 19 April* •

Today's eclipsed New Moon will bring you some breathtaking and life-enhancing opportunities during the rest of the month, so make sure you grab them with both hands when they come along. This is no time to be complacent or lazy because then you'll miss the boat. Instead, be far-seeing, positive and determined to make the best of whatever life strews in your path.

• *Tuesday 20 April* •

If you've been trying to unravel a financial problem recently and haven't got very far, give it another shot today. You might finally make contact with someone who can help you or who knows what they're talking about. There's even a chance that they might bend the rules slightly for you, but don't count on this happening as a matter of course.

• *Wednesday 21 April* •

You have a very high opinion of a certain someone today. In fact, they can do no wrong in your eyes right now and you'll adore being with them. If you've been hoping to turn a friend into a sweetheart, that's exactly what might happen now. You're in a very idealistic and romantic mood, but don't take that to extremes and kid yourself about things that will never happen.

• *Thursday 22 April* •

Be careful if you're going shopping with a friend today because they'll do their best to help you part with your money. They might encourage you to buy just about anything you see, probably because they want to feel better about their own shopping habits. Even though you want to enter into the spirit of the shopping trip, don't buy things purely to keep them happy.

• *Friday 23 April* •

One of the best ways to spend the day is to get together with friends. Maybe you could meet up for a drink or a meal with a chum, or arrange an impromptu outing with the gang. You'll also enjoy immersing yourself in a favourite hobby or leisure pursuit, especially if it allows you to express some of your many artistic talents.

• *Saturday 24 April* •

Watch out: power struggles are par for the course if you aren't careful today. There could be a clash between you and a loved one when one of you tries to gain control of the relationship or becomes very bossy. Don't be too quick to lay the blame at the feet of the other person because it's highly likely that you're both guilty of thinking that you know best. The more you press home your point, the more likely you are to have a gigantic argument.

• *Sunday 25 April* •

You're blessed with plenty of inventiveness and intelligence today, so don't let them go to waste. You'll be especially effective when trying to find solutions to bureaucratic or official problems, even if you can't put them into practice immediately. Today is also a good day to concentrate on your long-term plans or to map out your career path.

• *Monday 26 April* •

Do your best to monitor your words carefully; if you don't, you're in danger of dropping a brick or offending someone.

That might be because you're talking to someone who is ultra-sensitive or who takes political correctness to ridiculous degrees, but it's just as likely to be because your feet and mouth are showing an irresistible attraction for one another at the moment. Whoops!

• *Tuesday 27 April* •

If you're at work you'll be better off working by yourself because you won't like it if anyone tries to tell you what to do. They may think they're simply steering you in the right direction or giving you some valuable advice, but you'll see it as them being bossy, dictatorial or too big for their boots. If you're the one who's calling the shots, don't let power go to your head.

• *Wednesday 28 April* •

Thank goodness the atmosphere at work is much more harmonious and easy-going today. With luck, you'll be able to apologize if you think you went overboard yesterday, so there are no hard feelings. If you've been thinking about applying for a new job or putting in for promotion, your prospects are looking very favourable and it's worth sticking your neck out.

• *Thursday 29 April* •

If you want to make something happen, rope in a friend because they'll act as a catalyst for you. They might offer you the necessary encouragement or they may be able to pull strings for you. If you've been considering joining a club or society but have put it off through feelings of shyness, this is a good day to grit your teeth and take the plunge. What have you got to lose?

• *Friday 30 April* •

There's a very strong emphasis on the importance of friends in your life at the moment and today you realize yet again how influential they can be. A conversation with a chum will be inspirational and exciting, because they might give you some really good ideas or help you to turn a cherished dream into reality. Travel is also high on your list of priorities, especially if you're planning a holiday or pleasure trip.

MAY AT A GLANCE

Love	♥ ♥ ♥ ♥
Money	£ $
Career	🖥 🖥 🖥 🖥 🖥
Health	☼ ☼

• *Saturday 1 May* •

You're in a very decisive and productive mood today, which is just what you need to get ahead. Ideally, you should work by yourself as much as possible, because you'll enjoy your own company and you'll appreciate the lack of distractions from other people. It's a good day for concentrating on ways to boost your finances or to increase the amount of time you devote to some of your priorities in life.

• *Sunday 2 May* •

The atmosphere between you and a loved one hasn't been entirely plain sailing lately and once again you hit some stormy waters today. Rather than allow yourself to get swept along by all the emotional undercurrents, it would be far better to take a step back and try to work out exactly what's going on between you. Maybe one of you wants to make some changes to your relationship and the other is resisting them with all their might.

• *Monday 3 May* •

You have a choice: you can either continue yesterday's tension and moodiness or you can talk about it, preferably with the person concerned. However, do your best to avoid getting drawn into nit-picking arguments in which you simply get hot under the collar. Rather than argue about who did what and when, try to move forward and find some solutions to your current problems.

• *Tuesday 4 May* •

Today's eclipsed Full Moon is telling you that it's time to draw a line under part of your past, even though this won't be easy. You can't continue to live your life while looking back over your shoulder because it's preventing you from living fully in the present. It's also preventing positive new experiences from entering your life and enriching it.

• *Wednesday 5 May* •

Go carefully today as it will be hard to know what to do for the best. You might feel confused about your options, filled with doubt about your abilities, or defeated by the scale of the task in front of you. Don't let anyone make you feel worse by undermining you. Instead, pace yourself so you don't run out of energy, and take things one step at a time.

• *Thursday 6 May* •

Try to spare the time for a creative or artistic pursuit; it will go really well and you'll thoroughly enjoy yourself into the bargain. This is also a lovely day for being with someone special, even if all you do is share a cup of coffee or go for a walk. Pay attention to your hunches – some of them could be more accurate than you thought.

• *Friday 7 May* •

You won't always have as much energy and drive as usual between now and late June, and there will be times when you'd prefer to take a back seat. There will certainly be occasions when you'll need to conserve your energy or let others bask in the spotlight for a change, but try not to be reticent when it would be far more productive to make your presence felt, or to take action.

• *Saturday 8 May* •

Take care of yourself because you're in a fragile state right now. Your energy levels have dropped, making you feel that everything is too much effort, and also making you susceptible to any germs that might be floating around. You're also showing a tendency to worry and to let your anxieties assume monumental proportions in your mind. Come on, are things really that bad?

• *Sunday 9 May* •

You're feeling much more positive today and you're eager to make up for lost time. You'll be astonished by what you achieve if you're at work, and you'll also enjoy a nice sense of co-operation with colleagues and customers. Why can't every day be as good as this? You'll also get on well with older friends and relatives, especially if they have some good advice for you.

• *Monday 10 May* •

You're blessed with tremendous tact and diplomacy today, so don't let it go to waste. It's exactly what you need if you're trying to get back into someone's good books or you've got to take part in some tricky negotiations. A conversation with a friend will be great fun, and you'll appreciate one another's company even more than usual.

• *Tuesday 11 May* •

If you're trying to gain someone's co-operation or you're currently dealing with a big organizational project, today's events will be really frustrating and annoying. It seems that certain people are not playing ball with you and your plans aren't making much progress. There could also be a clash of opinions in which everyone concerned is determined to stand their ground. Stalemate!

• *Wednesday 12 May* •

Be wary if you're making some financial arrangements right now as you run the risk of getting carried away by optimism and enthusiasm. If you do, you'll waste time on making plans that will never see the light of day, perhaps because they're far too ambitious or because they overlook certain irrefutable problems. You can make progress now, but only if you're realistic.

• *Thursday 13 May* •

It's good news if you're at work because everyone seems to be batting for the same side and keen to create as harmonious an atmosphere as possible. As a result, you'll be able to get on with the job in hand rather than waste time or energy on keeping certain people happy. If you need some financial advice, today is a good day to ask for it.

• *Friday 14 May* •

If you want a nice, quiet day you should keep well away from any contentious topics of conversation. That's because certain people will quickly take exception to what you say, point out the flaws in your argument, or turn a conversation into a row. If you're furious with someone it will be better to say so than to engineer an argument about something totally different.

• *Saturday 15 May* •

You're in a serious and sober mood, and are showing a tendency to look on the gloomy side. Any problems that you're currently grappling with seem larger than life and almost insurmountable. Take heart: the situation isn't as difficult as it seems, even though you feel unable to deal with it at the moment. Give yourself a break and do something that makes you feel better.

• *Sunday 16 May* •

You've been doing a lot of thinking about your long-term plans and ambitions lately, and from today you should consider whether you'd be more successful if you added another string to your bow. Maybe you should retrain for a more lucrative career, or perhaps some of your existing skills could do with a brush-up? If computer technology is a closed book to you, maybe it's time to open it and get on to the information superhighway.

• *Monday 17 May* •

This is a terrific day for pooling your ideas with other people because you'll come up with some brilliant suggestions. You might be surprised by some of them, especially if they don't seem to be your normal style, but don't let that put you off. You're very inventive and clever right now, particularly when it comes to finding new solutions to old problems.

• *Tuesday 18 May* •

A certain person doesn't seem to have a clue what they're talking about today. They might get their facts muddled and cause confusion, or they could find it hard to stick to one subject for long. It may be tempting to get impatient with them but that will only fluster them still further. Besides, you may not be thinking as clearly as you'd like, either.

• *Wednesday 19 May* •

Today's New Moon is encouraging you to pull out all the stops if you want to make progress in your career. This is no time to tread water, put things on the back burner or take your eye off the ball, because that will lead to missed opportunities. You'll also be sending yourself the message that your ambitions aren't as important as you know they are. So get cracking!

• *Thursday 20 May* •

Although you've got a lot going on in your life at the moment, not least your need to pursue your goals, there will be times during the next four weeks when you'll want to channel lots of energy into your social life. If this is a part of your life that's been neglected recently, this is your cue to do something about it. Ring up old friends or join a new social circle.

• *Friday 21 May* •

Your brain is firing on all cylinders today, and it's coming up with some fantastic ideas. You'll be especially effective when thinking about matters connected with your career and your joint money matters. Don't worry if you've got to sort out some red tape because you'll slice your way through it in no time at all.

• *Saturday 22 May* •

You're eager to spend money on anything or anyone that means a lot to you today, and once you get the urge to do so almost nothing will be able to stop you. This is fine if you can afford it, but it isn't such good news if you're supposed to be going through a fiscally prudent phase. Prudence? You can't be bothered with such things at the moment.

• *Sunday 23 May* •

Life has kept you on your toes recently, so view today as the perfect opportunity to put your feet up and have a breather. You must admit that you aren't exactly feeling energetic anyway, and the thought of being busy doing nothing really appeals. However, if you're planning a romantic interlude with a special person it may not go the way you expect, so be prepared.

• *Monday 24 May* •

This is a wonderful day to get together with a friend and you'll get an enormous amount of pleasure from their company. You don't have to do anything very special, either, so don't worry if you can only spare the time for a quick cup of coffee with them. Anything is better than nothing right now. If you can't see them in person, give them a ring.

• *Tuesday 25 May* •

It's important that you know your limitations today, or you could be in for a frustrating experience in which things don't go the way you planned. For a start, you'll do better if you can work all alone because other people will distract you or put you off your stroke. If your current plans have to take lots of hidden or unknown factors into consideration, these might trip you up now.

• *Wednesday 26 May* •

Your emotions are never far from the surface today and it's important that you express them as much as possible. This might mean telling you-know-who how special they are to you, or it could involve picking up a paintbrush and creating a masterpiece. At some point you might also find yourself talking about a past relationship or resolving an old problem.

• *Thursday 27 May* •

Tread carefully with loved ones because they seem determined to do the exact opposite of what you want. If you were looking forward to an intimate evening with your other half, they might announce that they're going out with a friend. It's frustrating but what can you do about it? Go over any financial matters carefully to avoid making slapdash mistakes.

• *Friday 28 May* •

Be very selective about who and what you believe today. Someone may appear to be highly credible and trustworthy but you shouldn't take them at face value, especially if this is your first encounter with them. Do your best to be forthright with everyone, as sitting on the fence or hedging your bets will only lead to confusion and crossed wires.

• *Saturday 29 May* •

Make the most of your social life today because it looks really promising. Maybe you could get together with friends who you haven't seen lately, or throw yourself wholeheartedly into a local event. It's an especially good day for being with neighbours, particularly if you're hoping to improve your relationship with them. How can they resist you at the moment?

• *Sunday 30 May* •

It's another day when it's a pleasure to be with other people. You'll find it easy to get on their wavelength, even if you don't know them very well. Somehow you'll instinctively know the right things to say and do, so trust your hunches. These will also give you some important guidance about what's going on with a loved one.

• *Monday 31 May* •

If you're planning a forthcoming social event, you'll be very tempted to splurge on it to your heart's content. You might decide to increase the budget, even though you can't afford to do so, or you could be tempted to splash out on all sorts of delightful extras, such as expensive paper napkins or some impressive fireworks. Yes, it's good fun but don't spend what you haven't got!

JUNE AT A GLANCE

Love	♥ ♥
Money	£ $
Career	🖳 🖳 🖳
Health	☼ ☼ ☼ ☼ ☼

• Tuesday 1 June •

Someone is being very pedantic and picky today, as you'll soon discover when they correct you about all sorts of things you think are almost too petty to bother with. However, the boot might soon be on the other foot because you could easily become infected with the same attitude. If so, you'll waste a lot of time in unnecessary nit-picking.

• Wednesday 2 June •

This is one of those days when money slips through your fingers in no time at all unless you're very vigilant about your spending habits. Unfortunately, it will be difficult to stop yourself splashing out whenever the fancy takes you, whether or not you can afford it. You'll be especially drawn to tempting little treats and luxurious indulgences.

• Thursday 3 June •

During the coming fortnight you'll have to do some serious thinking about one of your favourite people. Maybe you need to have a quiet word in their ear about something, in the hope that you can nip a potential problem in the bud before it becomes serious. There's also a chance that your feelings for this person are changing and that you need to reflect on this and what it means.

• *Friday 4 June* •

If you're trying to make your money stretch as far as possible, today is a good day to discuss your ideas with someone who's financially minded and who can give you some useful input. It will also be helpful to bounce your ideas off them and use them as a sounding board. If you've been hoping to turn a colleague into a lover, work your magic on them now.

• *Saturday 5 June* •

The coming fortnight is an excellent time to think about your future plans. If they've hit some snags recently this will be your chance to work out how to get them back on track. You'll also appreciate the company of friends and anyone else who's on the same wavelength as you. It will be a pleasure to share your ideas and discuss your dreams with them.

• *Sunday 6 June* •

You have the happy knack of bringing out the best in other people today, so put it to good use. One of the best ways to do this is to sweet-talk someone into seeing things from your point of view, or to dazzle them with your charm if you suspect you've been rather off-hand with them recently. A group activity will be more enjoyable than you expected.

• *Monday 7 June* •

Yesterday's sociable atmosphere is increased today, making it a positive delight to be around you. This is just what you need if you're hoping to ingratiate yourself with a certain person, or perhaps convince them that they can't live without you a moment longer. They may not sweep you off your feet in the style of Rhett Butler, but they certainly won't ignore you.

• *Tuesday 8 June* •

What a fabulous June this is turning out to be! Today, you're blessed with oodles of charm and charisma, and you'll turn a few heads before the day is over. If you're currently a solo Leo, you stand an excellent chance of attracting someone wonderful now, even though they may start off as a friend. You've got the world in the palm of your hand at the moment.

• *Wednesday 9 June* •

It's a baffling day because you feel as though you're being bombarded by information from every side. Well-meaning people may be full of advice that you don't want, or everyone might start talking at once so you don't know who to listen to first. You'll also be aware of a perverse voice inside you that's telling you to do the opposite of whatever seems most sensible. Not an easy day.

• *Thursday 10 June* •

Steady on and take a deep breath. You're trying to do too much and if you carry on like this you're liable to fall flat on your face. There's nothing wrong with trying to cram so much activity into your busy schedule, unless you've set yourself an impossible task. Try not to make promises that you can't deliver or which will end up being very expensive.

• *Friday 11 June* •

The more eager you are to create positive change in your life, the harder it is to make it happen. Why is this? Perhaps a loved one is resisting it at all costs, even to the point of unpleasantness. Or maybe you suspect that something in you is secretly sabotaging what you're trying to achieve. Think it through carefully and try to find out what's going on.

• *Saturday 12 June* •

This is another day for enjoying your social life whenever you get the chance. If you weren't intending to do anything sociable today you might want to change your mind in order to make the most of this wonderful influence. Arrange a get-together with someone on the spur of the moment, ring up a chum or visit a favourite club and see who's there.

• *Sunday 13 June* •

You want to think the best of people today, and you'll do your utmost to give them the benefit of the doubt or to make excuses for them if needs be. This is a sign of your compassion, but are you sure they deserve such largesse? Unfortunately, there's a chance that you're fooling yourself about someone's motives or character, and are ignoring some nasty but glaring truths.

• *Monday 14 June* •

You're easily swayed by your emotions today, especially if someone plays on your sympathy or you're feeling guilty about them for some reason. In fact, it will be difficult for you to work out exactly how you are feeling, because you're in a confused and impressionable state. Be wary of anyone who might want to take advantage of your current mood.

• *Tuesday 15 June* •

If a relationship is currently undergoing a transformation, today gives you an excellent opportunity to talk about what's going on with the person concerned. You're in the mood for some in-depth and searching conversation. However, try to resist any temptation to brainwash or badger the other person into seeing things from your point of view, or even to insist that you're in the right.

• *Wednesday 16 June* •

If you're hoping that there will soon be some romantic developments with a friend, you'll have good reason to feel optimistic today. Even if you-know-who doesn't declare undying love, you'll realize that they aren't exactly indifferent to your charms. And who can blame them! Calm yourself down by enjoying a favourite hobby.

• *Thursday 17 June* •

Today's New Moon places further emphasis on your friendships and plans for the future, so you'd be wise to concentrate as much as possible on these during the rest of June. Make sure you're open to new ideas as well, because some of the concepts that come to you now will be far too good to ignore and you'll long to get started on them.

• *Friday 18 June* •

Let's hope you haven't got a busy schedule today because it will probably go for a burton once you start chatting to a friend. They'll have a tremendous amount to say for themselves and it will be difficult to prise yourself away, even assuming that you want to. Nevertheless, all social settings are ace now, helped along by your sunny and outgoing mood.

• *Saturday 19 June* •

It's important that you keep your feet on the ground today, especially where your finances and romance are concerned. But that will be much easier said than done because you'll have a strong tendency to get carried away by the heat of the moment, whether you're out shopping and spot something you've just got to have, or you're dreaming about you-know-who.

• *Sunday 20 June* •

You're in a very moody frame of mind and the slightest little thing could set you off. However, you'll deny this until you're blue in the face, and will probably blame everyone else for your outbursts of temper. Now, come on, Leo! Something is bugging you and it's making you quietly furious. Admit that it's happening so you can do something constructive about it.

• *Monday 21 June* •

If you're a typical Leo you usually enjoy being the centre of attention, but this won't always be the case during the coming four weeks. Instead, there will be occasions when you actually prefer to melt into the background and keep a low profile. You'll also relish the chance to spend some time alone once in a while.

• *Tuesday 22 June* •

Dare you let someone know what you're really thinking? You're in two minds about this, possibly because you don't want to shock them with your radical or controversial ideas. On the other hand, this really is a marvellous day for revealing a few secrets, provided that you choose your confidant with care and can trust them not to gossip about you to all and sundry. Or is that what you secretly wish they'd do?

• *Wednesday 23 June* •

Your energy levels start to rise from today, and they'll keep you in fine fettle until early August. This is a super chance to push ahead with any project that requires stamina, bravado or initiative, because you'll have bags of all three. Mind you, it's important to guard against any tendency to seem too brash, pushy or confident, so you may have to take yourself in hand at times.

• *Thursday 24 June* •

If you're already kicking yourself about those extravagant spending sprees you've been having lately, you'd better lock up your wallet or padlock your purse today. That's because you'll be overwhelmed by the urge to splurge and it will be almost impossible to resist it. If the shops are calling too loudly for you to ignore, take only the cash you can afford to spend and leave your credit cards or chequebook at home. Otherwise, who knows what will happen.

• *Friday 25 June* •

Once again the subject of spending money is never far from your thoughts. So put on a pair of blinkers when walking past your favourite shops, and don't imagine that buying things over the Internet doesn't count. Concentrate instead on giving your imagination some exercise, because it will come up with some very interesting scenarios and suppositions.

• *Saturday 26 June* •

Mix with friends and neighbours whenever you get the chance today. You'll enjoy finding out how they all are, even if you can only stop for a quick chat in the street. If, by some strange chance, your social diary is looking empty, it's a good day to put that to rights by making plenty of arrangements. If you can't afford to go out on the town, invite chums round to your place.

• *Sunday 27 June* •

Do your best to remain upbeat and positive today; if you don't, your mind will start working overtime and conjure up all sorts of worries. You're showing a marked tendency to view everything with deep doom and gloom, especially if it gives you the excuse to brood. Yet this is an excellent day for examining situations in a lot of detail, provided you can keep things in perspective.

• *Monday 28 June* •

Prepare yourself for some unexpected events today, particularly where close relationships are concerned. Someone might show a different side to their personality or make a declaration that catches you off guard. If an intimate partnership has been getting stale, start discussing how you can both liven things up a little.

• *Tuesday 29 June* •

Gather some of your nearest and dearest around you today because it will do you good to spend time with them. Cook them a meal or just have a chat over a cup of tea. You're in a reflective mood and your thoughts will soon stray to the past. You might even be tempted to get out some old mementos and have a poignant stroll down memory lane.

• *Wednesday 30 June* •

There is such a strong rapport between you and you-know-who today that there's almost no need for words. At times it will seem as though you're linked telepathically. Even so, it will be better to discuss things between you than to make assumptions about what the other person thinks, and then act accordingly. After all, you might be wrong or you may be confusing wishful thinking with reality.

JULY AT A GLANCE

Love	♥ ♥ ♥ ♥ ♥
Money	£ $ £ $
Career	💻 💻 💻
Health	☼ ☼ ☼ ☼ ☼

• *Thursday 1 July* •

Even the smallest incident could touch your heart today because you're in a very sensitive state. This is a great day for connecting with your real feelings about something or someone, but there's also the possibility that you might get all steamed up about things that don't really matter. So try to exercise a little discrimination and then things will be fine.

• *Friday 2 July* •

Today's Full Moon is pointing towards your general well-being and asking if you're taking as much care of yourself as you should. For instance, are you taking enough exercise to stay healthy or are you eating a good all-round diet? If you know you could improve this area of your life, start thinking about where to start. It's an especially good time to give up a bad health habit, such as nicotine or too much alcohol. Think how virtuous you'll feel when you've got this under control!

• *Saturday 3 July* •

It's one of those days when it's awfully easy to get caught up in silly details and nit-picking problems that distract you from what you really should be concentrating on. For instance, if someone's comments annoy you, you could get sidetracked by criticizing their grammar or general demeanour instead of analysing what's really bugged you.

• *Sunday 4 July* •

Over the coming three weeks you're going to have a lot to say for yourself! There will be times when expressing yourself feels like a matter of life and death, and you'll be very agitated if something prevents you from getting things off your chest. This will be a fantastic chance to air your views and opinions, but resist the temptation to dominate the conversation all the time.

• *Monday 5 July* •

You're capable of some small but powerful acts of kindness today, and you'll want to keep them quiet. For instance, you might drop some money into a collecting tin or write out a big cheque for a good cause, but you won't advertise the fact. If you're currently trying to make ends meet, consider applying for a benefit or allowance because you could strike lucky.

• *Tuesday 6 July* •

This is a terrific day for enjoying the company of cherished friends or partners. You'll hanker for people who make you feel safe, and who know you inside out. It's also the perfect day for being with one person in particular and making the rest of the world go away, as you create a romantic but seductive atmosphere.

• *Wednesday 7 July* •

Tread carefully with loved ones because conflicts or clashes look more than likely. Someone could get hot under the collar and raise objections to what you're trying to do, especially if it makes them feel threatened in some way. For instance, they may throw a possessive scene because they want to control your extracurricular activities and keep you by their side. You won't like it!

• *Thursday 8 July* •

You can achieve a tremendous amount today if you put your mind to it. You don't have as much energy as usual, but don't let that deter you from turning today's influences to your advantage. Ideally, you should have some time to yourself because you'll appreciate the peace and quiet, and it will enable you to do some serious thinking. You have abundant common sense right now.

• *Friday 9 July* •

Take it easy today because you're in a combustible mood and things will get under your skin in no time at all. You're also feeling sensitive and easily offended, which will cause problems if you're talking to someone who doesn't care what they say provided it gets a reaction. Wake up to the fact that they're trying to get you to rise to the bait – and they'll succeed very easily.

• *Saturday 10 July* •

You're feeling a strong sense of urgency about getting our point of view across, and you won't rest until you've said everything that you have to. This is ideal if you've got to stick up for yourself or defend yourself in an argument, but be very careful about sounding too blunt, forthright or downright rude. You may not realize the strident impression you're giving.

• *Sunday 11 July* •

Thank goodness you're in a much more diplomatic and easy-going mood today, so you can make amends if you think you went overboard yesterday. However, think twice before apologizing for what you said, because the only fault may lie with the way you said it. This is important if you were making some fundamental points about the way you want certain people to treat you.

• *Monday 12 July* •

Hold fire if you're supposed to sign an agreement or contract today, because things could easily go haywire. You might find that you've agreed to something that you don't want, the whole process could turn into a pain in the neck, or you could change your mind when it's too late to do anything about it. So make your excuses for the time being – it will be worth it.

• *Tuesday 13 July* •

Confusion is rife between you and partners today. This may not be deliberate, so don't immediately assume that someone is trying to mislead you. On the other hand, there is a distinct possibility that a certain person could be muddying the waters in some way or omitting to mention some rather pertinent facts that you really ought to know about. Proceed with caution.

• *Wednesday 14 July* •

If life has been a little fraught or difficult recently then it's about time that you had some light relief. So set aside some time for an activity that allows you to relax and forget about everything for a while. This might mean putting your feet up in front of the TV, going out for a drink with a friend or losing yourself in a favourite hobby.

• *Thursday 15 July* •

Take your other half by the hand and do something with them on the spur of the moment. For instance, instead of staying in you might decide to go out for a meal. If you're currently hoping that your relationship with you-know-who will develop into something much more intimate than it is at the moment, your dreams could come true now.

• *Friday 16 July* •

You're faced with more confusion in a relationship today, and there's every chance that it's a continuation of what happened on Tuesday. Be very careful, not only about someone else's motives but also about the impression you're giving. Resist the temptation to take advantage of this mixed-up atmosphere and cross the wires still further. That will really lead to trouble!

• *Saturday 17 July* •

You'll really enjoy putting your brain through its paces today, especially if you choose an intellectual pursuit. But don't be surprised if it's difficult to tear yourself away from it! It's a great day for trying your hand at a crossword puzzle or competition. You could also enjoy getting caught up in a detective story, whether it's in a book or on film.

• *Sunday 18 July* •

Personal concerns are of the greatest importance for you today and you won't really be interested in anything else. You'll try to steer the conversation round to yourself, whether you've got something important to say or simply want to tell someone what you had for breakfast. That's fine if they're willing to listen, but don't drone on if they've got things to tell you.

• *Monday 19 July* •

Take it easy Leo, or you'll end the day with steam coming out of both ears! You have a tremendous amount of energy right now and it needs to be released in positive and controlled ways. Ideally, you should do something physical because you'll definitely get ratty if you're too sedentary. If you're out driving, watch that speed limit!

• *Tuesday 20 July* •

A social event could work out a lot more expensive than you expected today, but at least it will be good fun. In fact, this Tuesday shows every sign of being one of the most enjoyable days of the month, and you'll tell yourself that you can't put a price on having fun. But you can, and the price you're prepared to pay for it may be more than you can comfortably afford. Boring, but it's a fact.

• *Wednesday 21 July* •

You're in a very practical mood today, especially if you've got to get your finances into some sort of order. You might be rather horrified by the amount of money you spent yesterday and realize that you can't carry on like this. Consider making a few changes to your financial arrangements, such as tucking away some money each month into a nest egg.

• *Thursday 22 July* •

You'll be blessed with extra self-confidence and energy during the coming four weeks, which is marvellous if you're hoping to make your mark on the world. But even if you've simply set your sights on wowing your own social circle, you'll be a massive success. This is also a great excuse for a change of image or a revamp of your wardrobe.

• *Friday 23 July* •

You're a magnet for friends and partners today because you're sending out such warm and considerate messages. So don't be surprised if someone decides to confide in you or makes it plain that they're one of your biggest fans. Even if you're just chatting to someone you'll be able to create a very cosy and safe atmosphere.

• *Saturday 24 July* •

Keep active! You have bags of energy and enterprise today and you'll want to make the most of them. If you're going shopping you'll have much more stamina than usual, and will also be good at striking a bargain if you get the chance. If you get involved in a discussion or negotiation you'll leave no one in any doubt about where you stand.

• *Sunday 25 July* •

Your finances will never be far from your thoughts over the next couple of weeks, so devote plenty of time to making sure that they're running as smoothly as possible. This might involve picking someone's brains, making some careful adjustments to your banking arrangements or simply taking more care over your spending habits than usual. It will all be good stuff.

• *Monday 26 July* •

Oh-oh, someone's in a paddy today. The better they know you, the less constrained they'll be about losing their temper. Such are the benefits of familiarity! Of course, there's every chance that you'll be the one who's hopping up and down with irritation, in which case make sure that you get angry about what's really wrong rather than about petty distractions.

• *Tuesday 27 July* •

Want to make a play for someone? Then do it today while everything is working in your favour and you're feeling nicely confident. But you'd better make sure you know what to do next, in case they give you the green light! This is also a lovely day for getting together with friends or for taking charge of a group activity.

• *Wednesday 28 July* •

Today is a great one for combining exercise and enjoyment in any way you like. You might want to confine your activities to the bedroom, or you could be tempted outdoors for a jog or tennis match. When dealing with loved ones, try to realize that your emotions are the driving force right now and could make you seem rather pushy or blunt.

• *Thursday 29 July* •

Your work goes really well today and you'll enjoy feeling that you're in control of what you're doing. At some point you could have an interesting conversation with a colleague or client, especially if it brings you closer together. It's also a good day to discuss a health matter with someone who knows what they're talking about.

• *Friday 30 July* •

You simply don't have as much energy as usual today, so you'll have to pace yourself accordingly. If you try to force yourself to do too much you'll simply run out of stamina at some point and have to admit defeat, which will make you feel embarrassed and possibly even slightly depressed. So do yourself a favour and take things gently for a change. Besides, you've earned a rest!

• *Saturday 31 July* •

If you're fed up with the way a partner has been behaving lately, you need to do something about it during the next two weeks. Maybe all the action you need to take is to have a quiet word with them and talk about what's going on between you. Alternatively, you may realize that more drastic action is called for, such as putting your foot down or even, in exceptional circumstances, walking away from the entire situation once and for all.

AUGUST AT A GLANCE

Love	♥ ♥ ♥ ♥ ♥
Money	£ $ £ $ £
Career	🖳 🖳 🖳
Health	☼ ☼ ☼ ☼ ☼

• *Sunday 1 August* •

It feels as though you're being bombarded with information today, making it difficult to know who to listen to first. This will be even more confusing if you're trying to straighten out a financial or official matter and everyone is giving you different advice. You're in an impetuous mood and could agree to something on the spur of the moment that you'll regret when you've had time to think about it.

• *Monday 2 August* •

A close partner could take you by surprise today, perhaps by making a suggestion that you can barely credit or by doing something that makes you see them in a new light. Although there could be some shock value in this, it will also help to liven up the day and give you something to think about. And you may decide that you like what they're suggesting, after all.

• *Tuesday 3 August* •

Be careful if you're going shopping because you're in the mood to splash out on all sorts of things. None of them may cost very much by themselves, but the total will soon mount up if you give in to temptation every time you see something you want. It will be hard to stagger home because you're laden down with so many carrier bags!

• *Wednesday 4 August* •

The closer you are to someone, the more likely it is that the atmosphere between you will be highly charged and slightly tense. Maybe one of you is feeling neglected by the other one, and you're craving their attention. There could also be a hint of jealousy or possessiveness in what happens between you now – proceed with caution.

• *Thursday 5 August* •

You long for a break from your usual routine, and you'll be counting the minutes until you can get away if you're about to go on holiday. This is exactly what you're in the mood for right now, so plan something else that you can look forward to if a holiday isn't on the horizon. How about arranging a weekend away or inviting a friend to come and stay?

• *Friday 6 August* •

You normally have a healthy dose of self-confidence but it could easily evaporate today, thanks to the dispiriting or ego-sapping behaviour of a certain person. You might suspect that they're looking down their nose at you or are deliberately trying to make you doubt yourself for some reason. This may be true but it might also be all in your imagination. So take care!

• *Saturday 7 August* •

Romance lights up your life during the next four weeks, much to your delight. You might experience this at second hand, perhaps because a loved one is walking around with stars in their eyes or because you'll revel in watching some soppy films. Alternatively, you could get drawn into a deliciously romantic phase with a certain person, and you'll be walking on air.

• *Sunday 8 August* •

You're feeling good, especially if you have to do something that puts you in the limelight or allows you to demonstrate some of your talents. You'll also be thrilled if someone you respect pays you a compliment or makes it obvious how highly they regard you. If you're out shopping, you could spot a status symbol that you long to buy.

• *Monday 9 August* •

Busy? You bet! The trouble is that there simply won't be enough hours in the day for getting everything done, and as a result you'll quickly get in a flap. Once that happens, spats and quarrels look more than likely, thanks to your lack of patience and the temporary departure of your sense of humour. But don't be horrid to people just for the sake of it.

• *Tuesday 10 August* •

If you're waiting for someone to repay a debt, do your best to chase them up during the next few weeks. You'll make it plain that you aren't going to let them get away with it, and you'll keep reminding them that you're waiting for your money. Money in general will be important to you, but don't let it make you unduly materialistic or acquisitive.

• *Wednesday 11 August* •

You're longing to be swept away by romance today, so you'll be putty in the hands of you-know-who. This is great if you trust them and you have a good relationship, but be wary of allowing yourself to be manipulated by anyone who may not have your best interests at heart. Right now you're feeling very idealistic and not able to protect yourself when necessary.

• *Thursday 12 August* •

Get cracking on creative projects today because they'll go really well. In fact, you could surprise yourself! Whatever you do now, you'll want to put your heart and soul into it so you'll feel cheated if you've got to do things that don't really matter to you. If this happens, make up for it in your spare time with activities that require your complete involvement.

• *Friday 13 August* •

Life is full of delicious surprises today, particularly when it comes to matters of the heart. Your beloved might sweep you off your feet all over again or persuade you to do something daring together. If you're currently unattached, your heart might miss a beat when you clap eyes on someone who's never appealed to you in the past. But they'll really get you going at the moment.

• *Saturday 14 August* •

This is a super day for assessing your values and priorities in life, and making sure that you're giving them enough of your attention. You won't be interested in simply passing the time with activities that don't mean much to you, and you'll also be reluctant to talk to people who you don't really care about. This may make you seem uncompromising, but so be it.

• *Sunday 15 August* •

Seize the opportunity for an in-depth conversation with someone who's on your wavelength. You'll enjoy talking to them and possibly even sharing some secrets with them. If you're hoping that this person thinks of you as more than just a friend, you'll get a good idea now of whether you're barking up the wrong tree or whether they reciprocate your feelings.

• *Monday 16 August* •

Today's New Moon is giving you the opportunity to introduce all sorts of exciting changes and improvements to your life during the coming fortnight. And if it's your birthday today, then you can look forward to a year of transformation and pastures new. Either way, the rest of the month is perfect for getting projects off the ground and showing how enterprising you can be in the right circumstances.

• *Tuesday 17 August* •

This is a terrific day for making some practical decisions connected with your finances. You know what you want to achieve yet you won't do anything rash and you'll also know when to stop. It's also a good opportunity to make a serious investment in something that will bring you a good return over the years, although you may want to keep it under your hat for the time being.

• *Wednesday 18 August* •

Someone is being very impetuous and daring today, and they're dead keen for you to join in. But should you do this? Although they'll do their best to encourage you, probably by minimizing the disadvantages and emphasizing the benefits, you should be wary of getting involved in anything risky, illegal or likely to cost you an arm and a leg. There is too much at stake.

• *Thursday 19 August* •

Once again you're being enticed to throw caution to the winds and do something reckless. You might be tempted if you're worried about being seen to be a killjoy or a stick-in-the-mud, but once again there are compelling reasons why you should avoid doing whatever is currently being suggested to you. Better to be derided as a scaredy-cat now than as a complete fool later.

• *Friday 20 August* •

You're taking a serious view of life today and have a tendency to worry about all sorts of things. Try not to keep these thoughts to yourself: they will only depress you and make you believe that things are worse than they really are. Instead, either confide in someone you trust or pour everything out on paper. You'll soon feel better.

• *Saturday 21 August* •

Keep on the move today because you'll enjoy making contact with lots of different people. What's more, being active will help to stave off any hint of restlessness or boredom that might otherwise steal over you. If you're going shopping it will be fun to take someone with you for company or to arrange to meet them afterwards for a drink or a meal.

• *Sunday 22 August* •

During the next four weeks there will be occasions when you'll be very interested in the value of things. This might be the spiritual value of a belief or activity that gives extra meaning to each day, or it could be the monetary value of your possessions. Although this is a good time to concentrate on your finances, don't do it to the exclusion of all else, or judge people purely by what they do or don't own.

• *Monday 23 August* •

If you're currently having a clash with someone over what both of you deem to be most important in life, try to talk it through now. There will be plenty to get off your chest but you must allow the other person to get a word in edgeways too, or they'll soon add that to their list of complaints.

• *Tuesday 24 August* •

Spend time with some of your favourite people today because you'll get even more pleasure from their company than usual. You don't have to do anything special, either – simply being together will be enough. You'll also enjoy expressing some of your creative abilities, and this will help you to get rid of any pent-up emotions that are currently bothering you.

• *Wednesday 25 August* •

During the next few days it will be almost impossible to avoid mix-ups and muddles, but try not to make the situation worse than ever by being unclear about what you mean. For instance, if you don't want to do something it would be better to say so loud and clear than to hedge your bets and pretend that you might be persuaded to change your mind later on.

• *Thursday 26 August* •

If you're supposed to be counting the calories at the moment or not allowing a morsel of fat to pass your lips, you'll struggle to keep to your resolve today. That's because you'll be very tempted by all those treats that are currently forbidden, especially if you feel in need of some emotional comfort. Giving someone a hug or listening to music will be better than raiding the cake tin.

• *Friday 27 August* •

A loved one could be careless of your feelings today, making what seem to you like crass or insensitive comments. Or maybe they're accusing you of something similar? It's difficult to keep a check on your emotions right now because you're in the grip of some rebellious feelings that demand to be expressed. But try to limit the damage as much as possible.

• *Saturday 28 August* •

If you're currently in two minds about your relationship with a certain person it will be even more difficult to work out what's going on today. For a start, you aren't thinking as clearly as normal so there's a chance that you might talk yourself into believing what you want to believe. You're also very susceptible to this person's charms and don't want to hurt them.

• *Sunday 29 August* •

Are you feeling agitated or annoyed about something? Then do something constructive about it; otherwise you're likely to take out your feelings on whoever happens to be around. This means you might pick a quarrel with them over something really silly, simply so you can let off steam. It will help to stay busy and physically active.

• *Monday 30 August* •

Reassess all your joint and official financial arrangements over the next two weeks, making sure that there are no loose ends waiting to trip you up. Are your tax affairs up to date? Have you paid your latest credit card bills? If you're fed up with the so-called service provided by your bank or building society, now is a good time to take your custom elsewhere.

• *Tuesday 31 August* •

Emotional matters are a minefield today. You're feeling so sensitive, and are so easily hurt, that you'll read all sorts of sinister motives into the behaviour of loved ones. Quite honestly, you might be better off by yourself until this tricky mood blows over, provided you don't spend your time brooding over imagined slights or nursing your grievances. Rejoin the world when you're feeling more positive.

SEPTEMBER AT A GLANCE

Love	♥ ♥ ♥
Money	£ $ £ $ £
Career	💻 💻
Health	☼ ☼ ☼

• *Wednesday 1 September* •

You'll do your utmost to ensure that everyone has a good time today. You're in a very considerate mood and want to put people at their ease. You'll be very charming, but take care not to give the wrong impression to anyone who might take advantage of it another time. For instance, you don't want to give the impression that you fancy someone if you don't really.

• *Thursday 2 September* •

Personal communications return to normal today after an irritating phase in which they've led to confusion and mistakes. You can get back on track now, and it's a good idea to check that any important letters or e-mails you've sent have reached their destination. If you've been toying with a decision, this is an excellent day for making up your mind and then acting on it.

• *Friday 3 September* •

If you're busy at work all your efforts won't be in vain because they'll come to the notice of someone influential. This is a good day for sorting out financial matters with the help of someone who knows what they're talking about. They'll soon put you on the right track and may also give you some valuable advice.

• *Saturday 4 September* •

You're fired up with energy and enthusiasm today, and want to get ahead with whatever is on your list of things to do. However, don't be so keen to get these tasks out of the way quickly that you end up doing them badly. It will be very frustrating to have to do something twice because you made a hash of it first time round.

• *Sunday 5 September* •

Watch out if a slight sense of superiority steals over you today because it will make you unpopular with whoever happens to be around. You may think you're giving them the benefit of your experience and wisdom, but they may interpret it as a sign that you're far too full of yourself. Be methodical if you're dealing with paperwork as you'll be likely to lose something.

• *Monday 6 September* •

Your powers of attraction are always pretty good but they'll be even better throughout the rest of September. If you want to make yourself utterly irresistible you could treat yourself to some new clothes or a different hairdo, but this will really be gilding the lily. It will also mean that if you set your sights on someone they'll be almost powerless to resist your charms.

• *Tuesday 7 September* •

Friends are great company today, even if you can only spare the time for a quick drink or a phone call. You'll enjoy chatting to them and you can always arrange to get together later in the week. If you're taking part in a group activity you'll welcome the chance to air your views while also allowing others to have their say.

• *Wednesday 8 September* •

You're tempted by the thought of impulse buys today, so be careful if you're supposed to be saving every penny at the moment. You'll do your best to hide your shopping by stashing it on top of your wardrobe or under your bed, hoping that no one will notice. If you're out and about you might have a surprise encounter with someone who always makes your knees go weak.

• *Thursday 9 September* •

You're feeling generous and could easily be persuaded to part with some cash if it's in aid of a good cause. Alternatively, you might decide that charity begins at home and that a loved one needs your help. If so, you'll have to offer your assistance in a way that doesn't make them feel patronized or as though the workhouse is only one step away. Be tactful!

• *Friday 10 September* •

It seems that you and a loved one are on a collision course about money or something else that you value. Unfortunately, neither of you is willing to back down or change your mind, so you'll soon lock horns. Be very wary about being drawn into power struggles today because they could get nasty, bringing out the worst in both of you. If you can't reach an agreement today, postpone the discussions until you're both feeling more amenable and flexible.

• *Saturday 11 September* •

You may be upset about what happened yesterday but this isn't the day to sort it out. Instead of being the dogmatic Leo you're now almost too eager to see the other person's point of view and keep them sweet. In fact, you're willing to agree to almost anything if it will prevent a row, and that might mean that the other person will take advantage of you in order to emerge the victor.

• Sunday 12 September •

If you aren't careful you could have a re-run of what happened on Friday, and once again you'll be determined to stick to your guns. Even if you know that this is a self-defeating way to behave you'll be powerless to do anything about it at the moment. You'll also be very resistant to change if you know that a relationship needs a rethink, and won't want to face up to the truth.

• Monday 13 September •

You're very prone to doing things on the spur of the moment today, especially when it comes to spending money. Those impulse buys may seem like a good idea at the time but you could soon change your mind once you get them home. Make sure you keep the receipts so you can take them back to the shop! Your other half may also want to make some confessions about their shopping.

• Tuesday 14 September •

If you're planning on making a major purchase you should try to get it out of the way during the coming fortnight because then it will benefit from the influence of today's New Moon. Even so, you should still consider whether you can afford it before you put your money where your mouth is, and it might also be worth doing some research to make sure you're getting a good deal.

• *Wednesday 15 September* •

You want to channel considerable amounts of energy into your priorities in life today and will get slightly narked if something stops you from doing this. You're also in a very assertive mood, so will have no qualms about making your mark on the world or putting someone in their place if you think they deserve it. That's fine, but don't go overboard and crush them completely.

• *Thursday 16 September* •

Follow up your hunches today because they're working well. However, you need to tread a fine line between acknowledging your intuition and indulging in any wishful thinking that might be going through your mind. In other words, resist the temptation to kid yourself about things that you know deep down will never happen in a million trillion years.

• *Friday 17 September* •

How is your new fiscal strategy going? Are you managing to keep down your expenses or make every penny count? At some point today find the time to assess your progress so far, and see if there is room for any further improvements. You're in a very realistic frame of mind, so won't commit yourself to any strategies that you know you can't manage, but nor will you make excuses for yourself if you haven't done as well as you expected.

• *Saturday 18 September* •

You're in a very dreamy and idealistic mood today, and your feet will barely touch the ground. If you're involved with someone then you'll only want to see the good in them, even if it's completely overshadowed by their faults. If a new relationship begins now it will always have strong overtones of fantasy and romance, making it hard to see what's really going on between you.

• *Sunday 19 September* •

This is a super day for taking care of the domestic chores because you'll get a certain sense of satisfaction from them. You'll also enjoy ministering to your nearest and dearest, perhaps by feeding them to within an inch of their lives or making their surroundings as cosy and safe as possible. You might also consider making some improvements to your home.

• *Monday 20 September* •

You're blessed with considerable tact and charm today, especially when talking to some of your favourite people. You might have a delicious but harmless flirtation with a friend or enjoy a wonderfully soppy encounter with your one true love. This is also a perfect day for going to the cinema or theatre, or visiting an art gallery or museum.

• *Tuesday 21 September* •

Once again you're in shopping mode and you'll jump at the chance to spend some big bucks, whether or not you've got them! This urge to splurge will soon be moderated but in the meantime you might decide to go for broke, so be careful. Nevertheless, you could make some very lucky purchases now if you keep your wits about you, but do watch the expense of it all.

• *Wednesday 22 September* •

Today is the start of a long phase during which all your communications will be emphasized. This means everything from the way you put across your ideas to your use of computers and telephones. During the coming four weeks you'll enjoy making contact with close relatives and neighbours, especially if this gives you the chance to offer an olive branch or two.

• *Thursday 23 September* •

You really shine in social settings today because you'll be so chatty and friendly to everyone you meet. You might even make a new chum in the process, so don't be shy about talking to people you hardly know. This is also a good day for visiting people who live a short distance away. You'll enjoy the journey as well as the visit itself.

• *Friday 24 September* •

Love has a life-enhancing effect today so don't underestimate its power. If you meet someone for the first time now you'll be completely bowled over by them and they'll have a tremendous impact on you. An existing relationship will also blossom, helped by your determination to increase the intimacy between you. You may also make a momentous decision about your joint future.

• *Saturday 25 September* •

One of the background influences of your life shifts today from money to the way you communicate with others, and this will affect you until October 2005. This will be a wonderful opportunity to spend more time with the people you see on a day-to-day basis, and to really enjoy the connections you establish with one another along the way.

• *Sunday 26 September* •

It will be almost impossible to stop you saying whatever is on your mind over the next few weeks, because you'll have such a burning desire to get certain things off your chest. It's wonderful to have the courage of your convictions, but take care that you don't become strident or bombastic in the process. You will also have to respect other people's right to disagree with you.

• *Monday 27 September* •

You're bouncing around and full of energy, so find as many outlets for it as possible. You won't be happy if you're cooped up in one place for too long and you might even get rather irritable. Daredevil activities seem very attractive right now but don't be too reckless, especially if cars or heights are involved. You must accept your limitations – otherwise you'll be in trouble.

• *Tuesday 28 September* •

The more convinced you are about the truth of something, the more you'll resist anyone changing your mind about it during the next two weeks. Yet it's important for you to be open-minded and receptive to a variety of ideas, especially if you're wrestling with a difficult decision. Be prepared to listen and learn, and possibly even to admit that you don't have all the answers.

• *Wednesday 29 September* •

The sky's the limit as far as you're concerned today. You're full of optimism and bravado, and you've got a lot to prove. This is a day when you can achieve a tremendous amount if you're sensible, but if you're foolish you'll fall flat on your face. Try to stop yourself making promises you can't keep, doing things that are beyond your scope, and saying things that you don't mean, and all will be well.

• *Thursday 30 September* •

Ideally, you should give yourself a change of scene today. It's exactly what you're in the mood for, and you'll relish the chance of a brief breather. You might even be inspired to arrange a longer break in the near future, such as a holiday or a weekend trip to somewhere you've always wanted to visit. It will feel great to have something that you can look forward to.

OCTOBER AT A GLANCE

Love	♥ ♥ ♥ ♥
Money	£ $ £
Career	💻 💻
Health	☼ ☼ ☼

• *Friday 1 October* •

You need patience when dealing with a certain person today because they're getting in a terrible muddle. They may not know what they're talking about or they could give you some misleading information. Yet you are also finding it hard to tune in to what's really going on around you, and have a tendency to over-emphasize things or convince yourself that a fantasy is fact. Watch out!

• *Saturday 2 October* •

This is one of those days when you feel you ought to cut yourself into several pieces in order to satisfy everyone's demands. One person may want you to go out with them, another may want you to stay at home and yet another may have something urgent to tell you. But you can't be in three places at once! Try to keep your cool and don't let the situation get to you. Everyone will have to take their turn.

• *Sunday 3 October* •

During most of October you'll enjoy life's little luxuries and treats even more than usual, and that's saying something. After all, if you're a typical Leo you love all the good things in life and do your best to make sure that you have them. But beware of being too self-indulgent during the next three weeks and ending up out of pocket because you've simply got to have whatever you want.

• *Monday 4 October* •

A loved one is taking things very much to heart today, and will create a tense and tricky atmosphere at the drop of a hat. They might engineer a row in which they can get a few grievances off their chest or boss you about in some way. Or are you the one who's behaving like this? If so, try not to let your emotions get control over you, making you do things you'll regret later on.

• *Tuesday 5 October* •

This is a fantastic day for creative and artistic activities which will bring out the best in you. They'll also provide you with a healthy outlet for your emotions, especially if you're still smarting over what happened yesterday. This is a super day for being with close relatives, neighbours and partners, because you'll create a very harmonious and relaxed atmosphere.

• *Wednesday 6 October* •

Go carefully in all emotional matters today because you'll encounter a few surprises. For instance, a partner might drop a bombshell that leaves you reeling, such as suggesting that you introduce more freedom into your relationship. If you're trying to get a new alliance off the ground, things won't go your way today and it seems the odds are stacked against you.

• *Thursday 7 October* •

Your spirits will plummet at the first hint of a setback or problem today, plunging you into a deep sense of gloom. This probably isn't justified but you aren't prepared to acknowledge that right now and will prefer to lick your wounds for a while. Try to snap out of this miserable mood by doing something that restores your faith in life.

• *Friday 8 October* •

You need a brief change of scene today. You'll jump at the prospect of any sort of outing, even if it's only a quick trip to the supermarket or a walk round the block with the dog. You never know who you might meet on your travels, and it looks as though there could be a very lucky encounter with a certain someone. Things are looking up!

• *Saturday 9 October* •

You're feeling sociable and outgoing, and the last thing you'll want to do today is to lock yourself away from everyone. Although you'll enjoy being with loved ones you'll be equally happy to chat to anyone else who happens to be around, and you could be drawn into an interesting conversation with a neighbour. Any local event that you're involved in will go well now because you'll put so much effort into making it a success.

• *Sunday 10 October* •

Cherished possessions have extra importance and significance for you today. You might enjoy polishing or cleaning some of them, or simply admiring them and congratulating yourself on owning them. Think twice before offering to lend anything of value because you'll be worried about it while it's out of your sight and you'll be heartbroken if anything happens to it.

• *Monday 11 October* •

A loved one is exerting some pressure on you, and from where you're standing it feels extraordinarily like emotional or moral blackmail. It's obvious that they want to bend you to their will but you don't like their methods. You will also baulk at giving them the satisfaction of agreeing to their demands, and worried that it will make them think they can lean you on any time they like.

• *Tuesday 12 October* •

You're in a delightfully expansive and gregarious mood today, and you're determined to enjoy yourself at every opportunity. This is bound to involve a lot of interesting conversation and you'll happily chat away for hours if you get the chance. That's great if you can spare the time but not such good news if you're supposed to be doing something else, such as work.

• *Wednesday 13 October* •

The best way to deal with any problems or misunderstandings between you and a certain person is to discuss them today. You're feeling forthright without wanting to be rude, and are keen to speak from the heart without covering your words in a layer of treacle. Be prepared to talk about what's happening between you and make sure you listen to the other person's point of view too.

• *Thursday 14 October* •

All your communications will go really well during the coming fortnight, thanks to today's eclipsed New Moon. This will be a terrific time to do some negotiating, or simply to discuss whatever is uppermost in your mind. It's also a great opportunity to arrange a short trip, such as a long weekend, that will give you a change of scene and a chance to recharge your batteries.

• *Friday 15 October* •

The next couple of weeks are a great time to talk to your nearest and dearest about whatever seems important at the time. If your usual conversations revolve around such mundane topics as what to have for supper, make an effort now to discuss deeper subjects. You might start talking about the past or finally be able to forgive one another for previous misdemeanours.

• *Saturday 16 October* •

You're in a quiet and reflective mood, so you'll welcome the opportunity to spend some time alone. Maybe you could go for a solitary walk, or tell the rest of the family that you don't want to be disturbed for a while. Your thoughts will start to veer towards the past, making you feel nostalgic but also offering you the chance to resolve an old problem.

• *Sunday 17 October* •

If you're currently thinking about ways to brighten up your home, you'll come up with some cracking ideas today. In fact, you'll be rather impressed with them because they'll show such foresight and ingenuity. Jot them down while they're fresh in your mind because it would be very annoying to forget them, especially if the brainwaves are coming thick and fast.

• *Monday 18 October* •

It's delightfully easy to get on well with everyone you meet today, whether they're best friends or strangers, and whether you'd arranged to see them or you bump into them by accident. You might even receive an invitation as a result, or be inspired to issue a few of your own. With communications going so well now, it's a good day for starting a discussion or negotiation.

• *Tuesday 19 October* •

Concentrate on mundane tasks because they'll go like clockwork. It will be really satisfying to get them all out of the way, especially if some of them normally feel like real chores. If you work from home, you could be inspired to do some tidying up or to rearrange your desk or files in a more efficient or ergonomic way.

• *Wednesday 20 October* •

Life could easily get you down today, so take care. You might be depressed by the turn a conversation takes, or feel fed up after listening to the news. You're definitely showing a tendency to look on the gloomy side and to imagine that things are worse than they really are. If you ask someone for advice, they'll be cautious at best and downright pessimistic at worst. So be prepared!

• *Thursday 21 October* •

Your emotions are like water today, flowing in all directions. This means that you're very susceptible to other people's behaviour and will be easily swayed by them. If they're happy, you'll be happy, and you'll be just as strongly affected if they're feeling miserable. Right now you're acting like a mirror to others, rather than being your own person.

• *Friday 22 October* •

You're feeling robust and energetic, and you've also got a strong urge to do whatever appeals to you. This may mean that you postpone something that you don't fancy doing so you can have more fun with another activity. You'll also be quite forceful when talking to partners, especially if you want to persuade them into seeing things from your point of view. But will you know when to back off? Let's hope so!

• *Saturday 23 October* •

A loved one is showing a marked tendency to rewrite history, and they're somehow kidding themselves in the process. Should you set them straight or allow them to indulge their fantasies? Be wary if you're buying or selling property because someone may not be entirely honest with you today, perhaps omitting to tell you some rather important facts or glossing over unfavourable details. Keep your wits about you.

• *Sunday 24 October* •

If you've been trying to push a grievance or resentment to the back of your mind, it will make its presence felt today. Or maybe it's a loved one who's so keen to dredge up the past? Either way, you should do your best to deal with the facts rather than indulge in emotionally charged accusations or dramatic scenes. These may feel satisfying at the time but they won't help the underlying problem one bit.

• *Monday 25 October* •

Someone is very full of themselves today. They're eager to blow their own trumpet, whether or not you think it's justified. They might also get carried away and exaggerate a little, so don't believe everything you hear. Make sure that you don't behave in this way yourself, even if it's very tempting to over-egg the pudding or put an extra gloss on a story. You'll be caught out!

• *Tuesday 26 October* •

If you're considering spending some money, today is the perfect day to do it. You'll be able to weigh up the pros and cons of what you're doing, and will manage to resist the temptation to spend more than you can afford. You might also end up with a really good investment that will grow in value over the years.

• *Wednesday 27 October* •

You have a lot of energy and will-power today, so use it wisely. If you discover that someone is easily influenced by what you tell them, don't take advantage of this situation to make them dance to your tune. Such a tactic will backfire on you sooner or later. Nevertheless, this is a marvellous day for putting forward your point of view without worrying about what others think of it.

• *Thursday 28 October* •

During the coming fortnight you should assess the progress of your career and long-term goals, to make sure that everything is going according to plan. If you realize that you've got stuck along the way or that your current ambitions are a waste of time, take some constructive action rather than just drift along hoping that the situation will somehow resolve itself.

• *Friday 29 October* •

You'll shine in social settings during the next few weeks so try to get out and about as much as possible. This will be a terrific chance to get to know some new people, especially if you've recently moved to a new area and are feeling a little lonely at the moment. Consider lending your support to a local enterprise or activity, or joining a neighbourhood campaign.

• *Saturday 30 October* •

If possible you should rearrange your schedule so you can devote plenty of time to your social life. It will be a joy to spend time with friends and family, even if you're only visiting the shops or sharing a cup of coffee. Someone may try to interest you in one of their favourite hobbies, and it might appeal to you more than you first imagined.

• *Sunday 31 October* •

A loved one is being bossy and controlling, and you don't like it. The more you stand up to them, the more determined they'll be to have the upper hand, and before you know it you'll be involved in a battle of wills. It may be much better to walk away from the situation until you've both simmered down. Otherwise you'll get drawn into some nasty mud-slinging.

NOVEMBER AT A GLANCE

Love	♥ ♥ ♥ ♥ ♥
Money	£ $
Career	💻 💻
Health	☼ ☼ ☼ ☼

• *Monday 1 November* •

You're blessed with plenty of vitality and enthusiasm today for anything that you want to do. You'll even manage to drum up the energy to tackle tasks that aren't exactly in your top ten but which nevertheless need your attention. If you're taking part in a local or neighbourhood activity, don't be surprised if you're asked to take a more dominant role in the future.

• *Tuesday 2 November* •

This is a really good day for putting on your thinking cap and planning any domestic projects that are currently in the pipeline. Your mind is running along very sensible and logical lines, so you won't want to waste time with any ideas that will obviously never see the light of day. There could be some good news from a government agency if you've applied for a benefit or allowance.

• *Wednesday 3 November* •

Someone is in too much of a hurry today, and as a result they're likely to work themselves up into quite a temper if things don't go the way they want. You might also be in a bit of a paddy now, especially if something is bugging you but you're reluctant to admit it to yourself. Don't take it out on whoever happens to be around, especially if they've got nothing to do with it, because that wouldn't be fair.

• *Thursday 4 November* •

Take care because it's difficult to know what's going on today, especially when it comes to relationships. You're absorbing the moods of the people around you, so you feel like a piece of blotting paper. You're also feeling very dependent on certain people and are reluctant to do or say anything that might make them reject you, even if this goes against your own interests.

• *Friday 5 November* •

Tempers are frayed and you're quick to get annoyed. That's because you're taking everything very personally and then reacting defensively to it, even if it doesn't really have anything to do with you. What's wrong? Something is obviously bugging you and you won't feel better until you've tackled it, even though you're very reluctant to do that for some reason.

• *Saturday 6 November* •

It seems that a loved one is taking a perverse delight in speaking out of turn or making announcements that send your eyebrows into orbit. It will be difficult to avoid reacting in exactly the way they want and going off the deep end. But if you stop yourself rising to the bait, you'll pull the rug out from under them and leave them feeling completely flummoxed. Then the joke will be on them!

• *Sunday 7 November* •

Life seems to consist of a series of hurdles and uphill struggles today. The more you allow these setbacks to affect you, the more downcast and annoyed you'll get. Do your best to take today's disappointing events on the chin, and to learn from them. Maybe a project isn't working out because it needs a rethink? If so, see what you can do about it.

• *Monday 8 November* •

Relationships are delightful today because you're happy to see the best in everyone and ignore their faults. Your social life is looking good, too, and might even lead to a romantic encounter. If you've recently fallen out with someone, this is the perfect day to kiss and make up because you have no desire to bear any grudges at the moment.

• *Tuesday 9 November* •

Today is a super day for chatting to loved ones and catching up on all the news. You're feeling very sociable and outgoing, and can think of nothing nicer than whiling away a few hours with a friend. You're blessed with a lot of charm today, so make the most of it if you're hoping to get back in someone's good books or persuade them to see things from your point of view.

• *Wednesday 10 November* •

Your emotions are heightened today and you'll enjoy talking about them to anyone who'll listen. For instance, you might have a delightful chat about your love life. It's an especially good day for talking to close relatives and neighbours because you'll find it so easy to hit it off with them. This is just what you need if you want to keep someone sweet.

• *Thursday 11 November* •

If you've been considering making some improvements to your home or garden, try to get cracking between now and late December. You'll be full of enthusiasm for the job in hand, even if it isn't usually your favourite occupation. However, beware of a possible tendency to insist that things are done your way or not at all. Some compromise may be needed.

• *Friday 12 November* •

If you're a typical Leo then your family means a lot to you. This might consist of blood relatives or it could be a collection of special friends, depending on your circumstances. Well, you'll enjoy giving them plenty of your attention during the coming fortnight, and there might even be an addition to the family circle. If so, you'll welcome this person with open arms.

• *Saturday 13 November* •

You're very alive to the nuances and subtleties of what people are saying today, enabling you to read between the lines and find out what they really mean. Or are you? Take care, because this is a day when it's easy to kid yourself and to hear what you want to hear in other people's words. Don't allow wishful thinking or prejudice to colour your ability to listen.

• *Sunday 14 November* •

Have you started your Christmas preparations yet? Not even thought about them? Then get out a notebook and start jotting down your ideas today. Once you get started you'll really get into the swing of it, and could come up with some really good ideas. You might even be inspired to do some Christmas baking, such as making the cake.

• *Monday 15 November* •

Do you have enough free time or do you feel like a slave to the rest of the family? If you long to have more time to yourself, start working out how you can manage it. Maybe you could get up earlier each day, or go to bed later. Or perhaps you should discuss your wishes with the rest of the family and, if necessary, set a few ground rules.

• *Tuesday 16 November* •

Leos have a reputation for being efficient and businesslike, and you certainly deserve yours today. You're working your way steadily through the chores, and doing so with a happy smile on your face. It's a very good day for working in tandem with others, whether this means pairing up with a colleague or roping in a helping hand at home.

• *Wednesday 17 November* •

Look after yourself because it's one of those days when you don't have as much energy as usual and it's affecting your mood. As a result, you're feeling depressed and lacklustre, and liable to make a meal out of any problems you encounter. Maybe you need an early night or a change of scene. Or maybe you need to sort out an underlying problem that you're pretending doesn't exist.

• *Thursday 18 November* •

Your social life looks promising today. Get together with some of your favourite people or take your partner out for the evening. It's a very good day to talk about whatever is on your mind at the moment and to discuss any problems between you. Keep the conversation light and easy-going, and really listen to what's being said.

• *Friday 19 November* •

Assess domestic plans from all angles today while you're in such a realistic and rational frame of mind. If some of your plans aren't working out in the way you want, you should devise a new strategy now because you won't be afraid to admit defeat and start again from scratch. If a loved one needs your assistance or support, you'll do your very best to help.

• *Saturday 20 November* •

A social event could turn out to be a disappointment today, perhaps because it doesn't go as you hoped or it's postponed until another day. Do your best to rise above all this, otherwise you'll tend to brood on what went wrong and assign all sorts of negative meanings to it. Resist the temptation to imagine the worst if someone is too busy to see you. It doesn't mean it's over between you.

• *Sunday 21 November* •

A loved one is being very forceful today and they'll make some very piercing and perceptive comments. You could get involved in a fascinating, in-depth conversation. If you've got some spare time you'll love reading a detective story or watching a thriller on TV. You might also do a little detective work of your own by trying to work out what a certain person is up to.

• *Monday 22 November* •

Between now and mid-December you'll enjoy doing some entertaining. Maybe you could throw a pre-Christmas party if you're feeling really ambitious? This might inspire you to make some improvements or embellishments to your interior décor, such as rearranging some of the furniture or splashing out on some new fixtures.

• *Tuesday 23 November* •

Have you made any plans for the Christmas holidays? If not, this is the perfect day to get started. You might decide to visit someone you haven't seen for a while, or even to arrange a last-minute holiday abroad. If such things are out of the question, consider organizing some day trips instead so you've still got something to look forward to.

• *Wednesday 24 November* •

Be careful when handling your finances today because you could easily do things too quickly and end up making mistakes that you'll kick yourself over when you discover them. If you suspect that an intimate relationship has become rather stale, consider how you can liven things up again, preferably with the consent of the other person. You don't want to spring any nasty surprises on them!

• *Thursday 25 November* •

Other people have a deep effect on you today, which may or may not be a good thing. For instance, someone you respect might swamp you with their advice and make you feel that you have no choice but to follow it. Alternatively, you might be entranced by the strong telepathic link that's flowing between you and a certain person.

• *Friday 26 November* •

Your feelings about a friend could change during the coming fortnight. They might do something that makes you angry or shows them in a totally new light, or you may realize that you'd like to turn them into a lover. Beware of rushing into hasty decisions without thinking them through carefully, in case you change your mind again.

• *Saturday 27 November* •

The shops are crying out for your attention and custom today and you'll get a big kick out of seeing what's on offer. If you can do some more Christmas shopping, then so much the better. You'll have some brilliant ideas about what to buy certain people and your considerable stamina will help to keep you going, even if everyone else starts to flag.

• *Sunday 28 November* •

Your emotions are pulling you in one direction and your thoughts are pushing you towards something very different today. As a result, it will be almost impossible to make up your mind about something. If someone is waiting for you to reach a decision, it would be far better to say that you can't do so at the moment than to plump for one option, then another, and then a third.

• *Monday 29 November* •

A relationship really blossoms today, bringing the two of you closer together and establishing an even greater rapport than before. You might even get an inkling of why you were destined to meet. However, you need to remain as realistic about this as possible, because it will be tempting to indulge in fantasies or read too much into the situation.

• *Tuesday 30 November* •

Between now and mid-December there will be the occasional crossed wire with loved ones. Do your best to avoid this by being as straightforward with them as possible. If you intend to throw a party soon, make sure there is no confusion about the date or venue. You may have to doublecheck someone's Christmas wish list to avoid buying them the wrong item.

DECEMBER AT A GLANCE

Love	♥ ♥ ♥ ♥ ♥
Money	£ $
Career	💻 💻 💻
Health	☼ ☼ ☼ ☼ ☼

• *Wednesday 1 December* •

Life seems a little bleak today but it's important to remain as positive as possible. This is probably just one of those days when everything gets on top of you, making you feel weary. If you do have something specific and urgent to worry about, it will be far better to take some constructive action, even if it requires a lot of courage, than to brood and fret.

• *Thursday 2 December* •

Your sunny temper has returned and you're determined to throw yourself wholeheartedly into whatever the day has to offer. Ideally, it should offer you some pleasure and laughter, so arrange something nice if you don't have anything planned. Your power to charm is considerable right now and it will make you a bit hit with whoever gets the full force of it. But don't give someone the come-on if you don't mean it.

• *Friday 3 December* •

Tread carefully if you're involved in a property deal or home improvement plan today because someone might try to pull the wool over your eyes. They might forget to give you some vital pieces of information, or give you the soft soap treatment in the hope that you won't ask awkward questions. You're very trusting right now but don't let that make you gullible.

• *Saturday 4 December* •

You're full of compassion and empathy for other people today, so don't be surprised if they come flocking to your side. You might even look after someone you consider to be a lame duck at some point. If you're a single Leo at the moment but have a huge crush on someone, some bewitching things could happen between you now so make sure you see them at some point.

• *Sunday 5 December* •

If there have been slight tensions or frictions between you and your nearest and dearest recently, this is the perfect day to get them out into the open, thrash them out and then forget about them. Things could get quite heated in the process but don't worry because they'll work out OK in the end. Put as much energy into kissing and making up as you did into arguing!

• *Monday 6 December* •

If you're worried about running up big debts in what is usually one of the most expensive months of the year, start keeping a running total of how much money you've spent so far. You might have to restrict the amount you spend on Christmas presents, or make other savings in order to stay within your budget, but you realize the folly of ending up severely out of pocket.

• *Tuesday 7 December* •

You're really on the ball today so there's no danger of anyone tricking you or fobbing you off with lame excuses. If you suspect that a loved one is hiding something from you, you'll want to question them in a lot of detail. That's all very well but try not to turn it into the third degree, or make them feel hounded or bullied by your desire to know what's going on.

• *Wednesday 8 December* •

Be choosy about who you spend time with today. If you're with someone who's habitually miserable or sorry for themselves, you'll soon be dragged down to their level and will struggle to recover again. However, you may feel such sympathy for their plight that you don't see you have any choice but to be with them. If so, do your best to remain positive.

• *Thursday 9 December* •

If you look closely, you'll see a black cloud hovering over a loved one's head. They'll find the smallest excuse for losing their temper or throwing a tantrum, so tiptoe around them or try to jolly them out of their filthy mood. If the situation continues you may decide that it would be better to get the inevitable argument out of the way than to pussyfoot around them any longer.

• *Friday 10 December* •

It's a wonderful day for being sociable, whether you're chatting to a loved one or going to a seasonal party. You're feeling very gregarious and will leap at the chance to catch up on all the gossip. However, be careful not to get carried away and say more than you intended. You should also stop talking every now and then so others can get a word in edgeways.

• *Saturday 11 December* •

This is another good day for socializing, and you'll manage to turn almost any event into an enjoyable occasion. What's more, you'll come up with lots to talk about, which will help you to get over any uncomfortable moments. If you meet someone who you'd like to know better, don't be shy about suggesting that you get together soon. Of course, they might beat you to it!

• *Sunday 12 December* •

Life will have plenty to offer in the way of enjoyment during the next two weeks, which is perfect if you want this to be a December to remember. Your popularity will be even higher than usual and you'll be in great demand. If you can spare the time from all your social commitments you'll enjoy starting a new artistic project or learning a new creative skill.

• *Monday 13 December* •

Stand by for fundamental changes in a close relationship today. Something that has been hidden or secret until now might come to the surface, forcing you to pay it attention. For instance, if you fancy someone but haven't done anything about it, the atmosphere between you now could become so torrid that you're finally overtaken by passion.

• *Tuesday 14 December* •

If a loved one is upset about something you'll do your utmost to help today. That might involve letting them talk about what's wrong until they feel better about it, or giving them your emotional support. Although you'll want to take their side, bear in mind that they may not exactly be giving you an unbiased report of what's happened, so you should keep an open mind.

• *Wednesday 15 December* •

If you're going to a festive party or gathering today you'll have a great time. It will be good to see some old faces and also nice to meet some new ones. Don't be shy about breaking the ice if you spot someone you'd like to know better. If you haven't yet finished writing all your Christmas cards, do your best to get them out of the way now so they aren't on your conscience any longer.

• *Thursday 16 December* •

You probably won't need any urging to do this, but the rest of the month is marvellous for being with special people and doing favourite things. You'll have a real capacity for pleasure and enjoyment, and you'll want to spread as much happiness around you as possible. Cupid could have you in his sights, so steer you-know-who under the mistletoe and see what happens next!

• *Friday 17 December* •

A loved one is being rather tetchy today. It won't take much to get on their nerves, even if you think they're being grossly unfair about it. Try not to make the situation worse by being sarcastic or provocative. Instead, encourage them to tell you what's wrong but without raising their voice. Once you know what you've done to irritate them you can start to put it right.

• *Saturday 18 December* •

If you were unable to resolve yesterday's difficulties they'll be even more pronounced today. It's important that you get everything out in the open so you can discuss it, otherwise you run the risk of harbouring resentments and grudges that will emerge further down the line. Be prepared to hear some home truths and also to deliver a few of your own. But be fair!

• *Sunday 19 December* •

Today you're capable of controlling your energy so that you only expend as much as you need at any given time. This will help you to keep going all day long without running out of steam. This is great news if you've got a lot to do. You'll be especially effective if you're busy around your home, perhaps making some final Christmas preparations or finishing off the decorating.

• *Monday 20 December* •

So far this December you've had to negotiate your way through the occasional misunderstanding with loved ones, but things return to normal today. Jump at the chance to pour oil on any troubled waters that remain, or make some other peace offering if you think it's necessary. If you've been wondering what to do about a loved one, you'll come up with the answer now.

• *Tuesday 21 December* •

Although the emphasis on laughter and leisure will continue during the rest of the month, from today you'll also have to pay attention to your working life. You might have to put in some extra hours in order to meet a deadline or you could soon be given new responsibilities. If you're fed up with your current job, start considering your options.

• *Wednesday 22 December* •

If you ask someone to give you a hand today, don't be surprised if they make a hash of it. That's probably because their mind isn't on the job, but it might also be because your instructions aren't as clear as usual. So before you get angry, check that what you said made sense. Relations with someone older or more influential than you could also be blighted by confusion or doubt now.

• *Thursday 23 December* •

The atmosphere is highly combustible today, with people getting in a stew about the smallest little thing. You will also have a tendency to get hot under the collar, especially if someone isn't doing things as quickly as you'd like. Try to stop yourself getting in a rage because once that happens it will be difficult to cool down again. Maybe you need some fresh air?

• *Friday 24 December* •

Perhaps it's the fact that it's Christmas Eve and everyone is busy, but you can't help feeling that you're walking on egg-shells around certain people. Their emotions are very close to the surface and could erupt at a moment's notice, perhaps in a storm of tears or a fit of pique. Calm them down and ask if you can do anything to help.

• *Saturday 25 December* •

You're in exuberant spirits today and determined to have as good a time as humanly possible. What's more, you'll want everyone else to enjoy themselves as well and will pull out as many stops as necessary to ensure that this happens. The wine will flow, the food will continue to arrive and you'll be the life and soul of the party.

• *Sunday 26 December* •

Despite the festivities, something is nagging away at the back of your mind and you won't feel happy until you've done something about it. Do your best to tackle it over the next two weeks while it will benefit from the influence of today's Full Moon. You know that you can't carry on like this for much longer, even if all you can do is change your attitude to whatever is worrying you.

• *Monday 27 December* •

It's going to be a super day! A loved one is making a massive fuss of you and it's doing wonders for your ego. You might fall in love with your current partner all over again, or a new relationship could get off the ground now in a haze of happiness. If things have been tricky with a certain person recently, you're now eager to bury the hatchet and start again.

• *Tuesday 28 December* •

You're in a sociable mood and will enjoy catching up with anyone you haven't seen recently. It will be great fun to have a satisfying gossip with them, and they could have some good news for you. Take the time to have a conversation with one of your favourite people: it will help you to understand one another better, which is always a good thing.

• *Wednesday 29 December* •

It's hard to pin down a certain person today because they're being so vague and dithery. Ask them a question and they'll vacillate or be unable to give you a straight answer. You might suspect them of deceitful goings-on but it's far more likely that they're simply in a world of their own and can't keep their mind on anything for long. Don't worry, they'll soon be back on Planet Earth.

• *Thursday 30 December* •

Today looks like being one of the happiest and most convivial days this month, so make the most of it. Ideally, you should make laughter and pleasure your main priorities, with a good dash of romance as well. Get together with people who always make you happy or devote yourself to you-know-who and indulge your senses to the utmost. You won't want the day to end.

• *Friday 31 December* •

There's an erratic quality to the day, with loved ones behaving in ways you hadn't counted on. The only way to cope with this is to be as flexible as possible. Someone might change an arrangement at the eleventh hour so you have to think on your feet, or they may be determined to do their own thing even though it doesn't suit you. Get any arguments out of the way quickly so you can enjoy your New Year's Eve celebrations with a glad heart.

YOUR LEO SUN SIGN

In this chapter I am going to tell you all about your Leo Sun sign. But what is a Sun sign? It often gets called a star sign, but are they the same thing? Well, yes, although 'Sun sign' is a more accurate term. Your Sun sign is the sign that the Sun occupied when you were born. Every year, the Sun moves through the heavens and spends an average of 30 days in each of the twelve signs. When you were born, the Sun was moving through the sign of Leo, so this is your Sun or star sign.

This chapter tells you everything you want to know about your Sun sign. To start off, I describe your general personality – what makes you tick. Then I talk about your attitude to relationships, the way you handle money, what your Sun sign says about your health and, finally, which careers are best for you. Put all that together and you will have a well-rounded picture of yourself.

Character

Leo is the zodiac sign connected with royalty, and there's always something regal about a Leo. It may be your dignified manner, your air of calm authority or perhaps it's the tiara perched on your head! It's an entirely fitting association, though, because Leo is the sign of the lion, and what is the lion but the king of the jungle? Many words connected with lions also apply to Leos. You have a lot of pride, for instance, and it's often completely justified. You may also have a mane of hair, just like your feline counterpart. Very often a Leo is easily identifiable by their hair and, in suitably royal style, it's often referred to as their crowning glory!

If you're a typical Leo, you must admit that you like being in the limelight every now and then. You may not want to be the centre of attention twenty-four hours a day (although some Leos do), but you certainly like people to take notice of you. You aren't comfortable with the idea of playing second fiddle to someone, and even if you are initially happy to be in someone's shadow you soon want to emerge into the limelight yourself.

Leos like things to be done properly and you're certainly fantastic at organizing people and making systems run smoothly. Sometimes you may have a tendency to switch from being a good organizer to someone who's a bit bossy and who thinks they know best. Not surprisingly, this isn't very popular with other people!

Relationships

A Leo without someone to love is like a bird without feathers. You wouldn't know what to do with yourself! Actually, love is one of your specialities and you spend a lifetime working on getting it right. You have a natural gift for love in all its forms, from heady romance to enduring friendship, from parental care to sibling affection, plus many other categories along the way.

Your tremendous loyalty is one of the reasons you excel at relationships. People know they can rely on you and your Leo pride won't allow you to let them down. Of course, there are times when you can't fulfil people's expectations of you and these will really worry you. You'll feel you haven't done your best, even when you have.

A happy family is very important to you. Like any self-respecting lion, you like to be surrounded by cubs, so you enjoy having children around. You also enjoy having a partner you can depend on. You place a strong emphasis on fidelity and will be bitterly hurt if you discover your partner has been unfaithful. It's something you would find hard to understand – and to forgive.

You belong to the element of Fire, making you enthusiastic, affectionate and loving. Being demonstrative comes naturally to you, and you're very expansive with the ones you love. You also enjoy buying them little treats and huge gifts when the money allows. It gives you great pleasure to choose items that you know they'll like. And you're thrilled when they do the same for you.

Money

This is often a sore point for you! Your innate generosity and your appreciation for all the good things in life mean you're frequently out of pocket. Even if you earn good money, it can all vanish in delicious spending sprees and trips to your favourite restaurants. You like the idea of picking up the tab for things because it means you're taking care of people and making them feel good. But it can lead to hideous credit card bills or bright red bank accounts. What's more, you like to do things properly, so you will want to give someone the very best that you can afford.

If you're honest, you'll admit that you like the idea of having money. You enjoy the cachet it brings and the things it can buy. For instance, given the choice between staying in a luxurious hotel and roughing it in a bed and breakfast, guess which one you're going to choose! You have this approach to everything in life, and you believe that quality rather than quantity wins every time. Why buy something shoddy when you can save up your money and buy the real thing? No wonder gold is your colour!

If you've got some spare cash and are looking for interesting ways to invest it, you might be attracted to antique jewellery. Made from gold, of course!

Health

Your element of Fire and your ruling planet, the Sun, give you plenty of energy but it can burn out quite quickly sometimes. You can run out of steam, especially if you feel your efforts aren't being appreciated. Your energy levels can also be depleted when your relationships aren't going according to plan.

Leo rules two areas of the body – the heart and the spine. Since all Leos have big hearts, it makes sense that your sign rules this particular muscle. However, it does mean you need to take care of your heart. You might be interested in eating a diet that is good for your heart and in taking plenty of regular cardiovascular exercise.

It's very important that you learn to take care of your back too, since this is the other area that's vulnerable for Leos. Ideally, you should learn how to lift heavy objects without placing a lot of strain on your spine, and choose chairs that support your back rather than allow it to go into a slump. You should also make sure you're sleeping on a good mattress.

Exercise is good for all of us but is especially good for you because it allows you to express yourself – something that is essential to any Leo's mental and emotional health. If you don't fancy working up a sweat in the gym, consider taking up dancing, skating or any other sport that combines balletic grace with muscle power. You'll enjoy yourself so much that you won't want to stop!

Career

To put it simply, anything creative is right up your street! Your most important need, when looking for a job, is something that will enable you to express yourself and put some of your many talents to good use. You hate the thought of having to do a job simply because it pays the bills and for no other reason. Ideally, you want something that gives you some scope and in which you can be proud of your efforts.

Creativity comes in many forms, of course. You might feel drawn to one of the artistic professions that are especially suited to Leos, such as dancing, singing or painting. Or you may fancy testing out your dramatic skills – Hollywood and the theatre are studded with Leos!

Whatever you do for a living, you'll soon take charge of things and try to organize them as efficiently as possible. You may also have your eye on the top job, which can make your boss feel rather uncomfortable!

LOVE AND THE STARS

Have you ever noticed that you get on better with some signs than others? Perhaps all your friends belong to only a few signs or you've never hit it off with people who come from a particular sign. Or maybe you've recently met someone from a sign that you aren't familiar with at all, and you're wondering how your relationship will develop. Well, this chapter gives you a brief insight into your relationship with the other Sun signs. Check the combination under your own sign's heading first, then read about your relationship from the viewpoint of the other sign to find out what they think of you. It could be very revealing!

At the end of this chapter you'll find two compatibility charts that tell you, at a glance, how well you get on with the other signs as lovers and as friends. Look for the woman's Sun sign along the top of the chart and then find the man's sign down the side. The box where the two meet will show how well they get on together.

Even if your current relationship gets a low score from the charts, that doesn't mean it won't last. It simply indicates that you'll have to work harder at this relationship than at others.

Leo

Leo and **Leo** is a very strong combination but there could be a few battles for power every now and then. After all, neither of you likes to relinquish the reins and hand over control to anyone else. Even so, you'll have a lot of fun.

Leo and **Virgo** is fine if you're prepared for some give and take but it won't be very easy if each of you stands your ground. You'll be pleased if your Virgo tries to help or advise you, but will be hurt if this turns to undue criticism.

Leo and **Libra** is a delicious pairing because it brings together the two signs of love. You'll adore being with someone who is so considerate, although their lack of decisiveness may sometimes make you grit your teeth with irritation.

Leo and **Scorpio** is wonderful until you have a row. At that point, you'll both refuse to budge an inch and admit that you might be in the wrong. You both set a lot of store by status symbols, which could work out expensive.

Leo and **Sagittarius** is great for keeping each other amused. You're both enthusiastic, intuitive and expansive, although you could sometimes be annoyed if your Sagittarian's social life prevents you seeing much of them.

Leo and **Capricorn** share a tremendous love of family and you'll enjoy creating a happy home together. Don't expect your Capricorn to be instinctively demonstrative: you may have to teach them to be more open.

Leo and **Aquarius** understand each other even if you don't always see eye to eye. Sometimes you can be left speechless by your plain-speaking Aquarian, and disappointed by their occasional reluctance to be cuddly.

Leo and **Pisces** bring out each other's creativity. This is a superb artistic partnership but may not be such good news if you're trying to maintain a sexual relationship because you have so little in common.

Leo and **Aries** have terrific fun together and will share many adventures. You'll enjoy making lots of plans, even if they don't always work out. You'll also spend plenty of money on lavishly entertaining your friends.

Leo and **Taurus** is the sort of relationship that makes you feel you know where you stand. You love knowing that your Taurean is steadfast and true, and that together you make a formidable team.

Leo and **Gemini** is a fun-filled combination that you really enjoy. You're stunned by your Gemini's endless inventiveness and their versatility, although you may secretly believe that they spread themselves too thin.

Leo and **Cancer** is great if you both need a comfortable and cosy home. But you may soon feel hemmed in if your Cancerian wants to restrict your social circle to nothing but family and close friends. You need more scope than that.

Virgo

Virgo and **Virgo** can endure many storms together, even though it's tough going at times. Here is someone who completely understands your interesting mixture of quirky individualism and the need to conform.

Virgo and **Libra** get on well together up to a point but can then come unstuck. It annoys you when your Libran fails to stand up for themselves and you don't understand why they're so touchy when you point out their faults.

Virgo and **Scorpio** are both fascinated by the details of life and you'll spend many happy hours analysing people's characters. Try not to be too brusque when pointing out some of your Scorpio's stranger points; they won't like it!

Virgo and **Sagittarius** is a very sociable pairing and you'll enjoy being together. You'll also have some fascinating conversations in which you both learn a lot. Sexually, it will either be great or ghastly.

Virgo and **Capricorn** really understand each other. You appreciate your Capricorn's reliability but worry about their workaholic tendencies. You'll both benefit from being openly affectionate and loving with one another.

Virgo and **Aquarius** enjoy discussing just about everything under the sun. But you'll quickly get irritated by your Aquarian's idiosyncratic views and their insistence that they're always right. Surely if anyone's right, you are?

Virgo and **Pisces** is not the easiest combination you can choose. If your Piscean finds it hard to face up to reality, you won't be sympathetic because you simply can't understand such an ostrich-like attitude.

Virgo and **Aries** struggle to get on well as close partners. You simply don't understand each other. They make a mess and you like things to be tidy. They rush into things and you like to take your time. There is little common ground.

Virgo and **Taurus** love each other's company. You both like to keep your feet on the ground and you share a healthy respect for money. You also have a very raunchy time in the bedroom although you don't advertise that fact.

Virgo and **Gemini** is a super combination for friendship or business. You think along similar lines and both excel at being flexible. However, in a sexual relationship you may fail to appreciate each other's finer points.

Virgo and **Cancer** is a great team. You like to take care of worldly matters while your Cancerian creates a happy and cosy home. If they collect a lot of clutter you'll think of it as dust traps rather than delightful keepsakes.

Virgo and **Leo** find it hard to understand each other because you're so different. You may secretly find your Leo rather ostentatious and there could be rows about the amount of money they spend. Try to live and let live.

Libra

Libra and **Libra** get on really well provided at least one of you is decisive and able to say what they think sometimes. You'll appreciate one another's consideration, sensitivity and intelligence. A great combination!

Libra and **Scorpio** are good friends but may not understand each other's sexual and emotional needs. You may feel uncomfortable with the brooding, intense moods of your Scorpio, wishing they took things less seriously.

Libra and **Sagittarius** have lots of fun together, especially when it comes to discussing ideas and taking off on jaunts. However, you could be rather nonplussed, and possibly even hurt, by your Sagittarian's blunt comments.

Libra and **Capricorn** get on famously if you share goals. You understand each other's need to work hard towards your ambitions. But you'll have to coax your Capricorn into being as demonstrative and loving as you'd like.

Libra and **Aquarius** appreciate one another's minds. You may be better friends than lovers, because you could be bemused and hurt if your Aquarian is unnerved by your need for romance and idealism.

Libra and **Pisces** share a need for peace and harmony. You'll adore being with someone who's so artistic and sensitive, but you both need to balance your romantic natures with hefty doses of reality every now and then.

Libra and **Aries** are a great example of how opposites can attract. You admire the way your brave Arien can be so outspoken, and they may even manage to teach you to stand up for yourself.

Libra and **Taurus** share a love of beauty and an appreciation of the finer things in life. At first you may think you've found your perfect partner, although you may get irritated if your Taurean is very placid.

Libra and **Gemini** get on well in every sort of relationship. You're amused by your Gemini's butterfly ability to flit from one topic to the next and will enjoy encouraging them to discover the romance that lurks inside them.

Libra and **Cancer** enjoy one another's company. You love the way your Cancerian so obviously cares about your welfare and happiness, and it does you good to be the one who's fussed over for a change.

Libra and **Leo** can be a very expensive combination! Neither of you is frightened to spend money and together you can have a field day. Emotionally, you revel in one another's company because you're both born romantics.

Libra and **Virgo** have to make a lot of effort to appreciate one another. You can understand the importance of attending to details but you may secretly think that your Virgo sometimes is too much of a nit-picker.

Scorpio

Scorpio and **Scorpio** feel safe with each other. You both know what you're capable of, good and bad. It's great to be with someone who matches you for intensity, but you might wind each other up and feed each other's neuroses.

Scorpio and **Sagittarius** can miss each other by miles. Even as friends, it's hard to understand one another. You like to zero in on the details while your Sagittarian prefers to take a broad view of the entire situation.

Scorpio and **Capricorn** bring out the best in one another, but it can take a little time. You enjoy the serious side to your Capricorn but you can also have some great laughs together. You also love knowing that they're so reliable.

Scorpio and **Aquarius** can have some terrific rows! You both have a tendency to be dogmatic and it's even worse when you get together. You can feel threatened if your Aquarian isn't as openly affectionate as you'd like.

Scorpio and **Pisces** share some powerful moments together. You love the complexity and sensitivity of your Piscean but will soon become suspicious if you think they're holding out on you or are playing games behind your back.

Scorpio and **Aries** is a tempestuous combination. Your temper builds up from a slow burn while your Arien will have a quick tantrum and then forget about it. Sexually, you'll have more than met your match.

Scorpio and **Taurus** complement each other in many ways. You're both loyal and loving, and you both need a secure home. However, problems will arise if one or both of you is possessive and jealous.

Scorpio and **Gemini** hit it off as friends but will struggle to stick together as lovers. You like to explore the nitty-gritty of situations while your Gemini apparently prefers to skim the surface. You may wonder if you can trust them.

Scorpio and **Cancer** can enjoy a highly emotional and satisfying relationship. You understand one another's needs and will take great delight in creating a stable and happy home life together.

Scorpio and **Leo** is tricky if you both want to rule the roost. Neither of you likes to relinquish control of situations, which can lead to some stormy battles for power. At times you may be jealous of your Leo's huge circle of friends.

Scorpio and **Virgo** have some wonderfully analytical conversations. You both enjoy digging below the surface to find out what's really going on. If it's a sexual relationship, its success will rest on what happens in the bedroom.

Scorpio and **Libra** appreciate one another but you may sometimes wish your Libran could be more forceful and dynamic. It will drive you mad when they sit on the fence or bend over backwards to please everyone.

Sagittarius

Sagittarius and **Sagittarius** will either have a whale of a time or never see each other. If you both have wide-ranging interests, it may be difficult to make enough time for one another and you may eventually drift apart.

Sagittarius and **Capricorn** think of each other as a creature from another planet. You like your Capricorn's common sense but will soon get fed up if they cling to tradition, are a workaholic or never want to take any risks.

Sagittarius and **Aquarius** have a fantastic time together. You share so many interests that there is always something to talk about, with some far-ranging discussions. But you may wish your Aquarian were less pedantic.

Sagittarius and **Pisces** enjoy being friends but it can be difficult to understand each other as lovers. You like your Piscean's sensitivity but wish they weren't quite so easily hurt when you make off-the-cuff comments.

Sagittarius and **Aries** is great fun. You'll have all sorts of adventures together, with exotic holidays a particular indulgence. You're both pretty outspoken and your no-holds-barred rows will raise the roof.

Sagittarius and **Taurus** struggle to hit it off. You're so different that it's hard to find much common ground. If your Taurean is possessive, you'll soon feel trapped and want to break free, or decide to do things behind their back.

Sagittarius and **Gemini** is a super combination. You have masses in common and are endlessly intrigued by one another. However, you must be friends as well as lovers, otherwise you may soon get bored with each other.

Sagittarius and **Cancer** can't make each other out at all. You're mystified by your Cancerian's constant need for their home and family, and will be irritated if you think they're too parochial and unadventurous.

Sagittarius and **Leo** revel in each other's company, especially when it comes to having fun. This can be an expensive pairing because you both enjoy living it up whenever you get the chance. Shopping trips will also be costly.

Sagittarius and **Virgo** is OK up to a point. You enjoy each other's brains but you'll soon lose patience if your Virgo is very finicky and anxious. You like to let your hair down but they may always worry about the consequences.

Sagittarius and **Libra** like each other, whether as friends, family or lovers. You have enough similarities to find some common ground but enough differences to keep things interesting. It's an intriguing combination.

Sagittarius and **Scorpio** try and fail to understand each other. You like to take life as it comes and can't stand your Scorpio's tendency to plot things in advance. You'll hate it if they're suspicious or jealous of you.

Capricorn

Capricorn and **Capricorn** feel very safe together. At last you're with someone who understands you, and who's as reliable and responsible as you. However, this may mean that your work clashes with your relationship.

Capricorn and **Aquarius** is either a big hit or a big no-no. You both need to compromise and be willing to learn from each other for it to work. Your love of convention will be sorely challenged by your radical Aquarian.

Capricorn and **Pisces** can learn a lot from each other as friends. You'll learn to be more sensitive and open-minded. However, you'll soon be turned off if your Piscean is reluctant to face up to facts and be realistic.

Capricorn and **Aries** support each other in many ways. You're both ambitious and will respect one another's goals. You'll enjoy teaching your Arien to be more responsible, and they'll teach you how to play.

Capricorn and **Taurus** feel safe with one another. You both understand the importance of tradition and share the need to do things properly. You can get surprisingly earthy and intense in the bedroom.

Capricorn and **Gemini** don't really hit it off. You're amused by your Gemini but you may secretly think they're too flighty and superficial for you. It's difficult to find much common ground sexually or emotionally.

Capricorn and **Cancer** really enjoy each other's company. You both adore having someone to take care of, and if anyone can dissuade you from working round the clock it's a home-cooking, sensuous and affectionate Cancerian.

Capricorn and **Leo** both like the best in life but you won't be as willing to pay for it as your Leo. In fact, you may be seriously worried by their extravagance and also slightly wearied by their demanding social life.

Capricorn and **Virgo** go together like bread and butter. However, there may not be much jam if you're both careful with your money. If you share a home you'll want it to be traditional, with conventional family values.

Capricorn and **Libra** have a healthy respect for each other. You love your Libran's diplomacy and tact, because you know you can take them anywhere and they'll fit in. They'll also encourage you to open up emotionally.

Capricorn and **Scorpio** is a very businesslike pairing. You excel at making money together, no matter what your relationship. Sometimes you can be put off by the intense and complex passions of your Scorpio.

Capricorn and **Sagittarius** can be strange. You like each other for your curiosity value if not much else. Even so, your Sagittarian will teach you to be more broad-minded and relaxed, if you let them.

Aquarius

Aquarius and **Aquarius** is either wonderful or too much like hard work. One if not both of you must be willing to compromise sometimes, otherwise it will be continual stalemate. You'll have formidable battles of intellect.

Aquarius and **Pisces** is tricky. You don't understand each other, and the more unworldly and unrealistic your Piscean, the more dogmatic and precise you'll become in retaliation. You can easily hurt each other.

Aquarius and **Aries** are great sparring partners and you'll love every minute of it. Your Arien isn't afraid to stand up to you and to fight their corner. They'll also teach you a thing or two about sexual relationships.

Aquarius and **Taurus** is fine all the while you agree with each other. But at the first hint of dissent, it will be war. Your need for emotional and intellectual freedom will clash with your Taurean's need for closeness.

Aquarius and **Gemini** are firm friends. You enjoy intense intellectual discussions and your Gemini will teach you to be more free-thinking and flexible. Try not to analyse your relationship out of existence.

Aquarius and **Cancer** can be an uneasy combination. You have little in common and don't understand each other. At first you'll enjoy being taken care of by your Cancerian but you may soon feel suffocated and trapped.

Aquarius and **Leo** enjoy each other's company. You love your Leo's exuberance and marvel at their social skills. You'll also be very impressed by their ability to organize you and make your life run so smoothly.

Aquarius and **Virgo** can seem like hard work. It's easier to be friends than lovers because you have such different views of the world. You enjoy pitting your wits against each other in wide-ranging discussions.

Aquarius and **Libra** is great fun and you love sharing ideas. If you get involved in an emotional relationship, your Libran will encourage you to be more demonstrative and less analytical about your feelings.

Aquarius and **Scorpio** is a very powerful combination because you're both so sure of yourselves. In the inevitable disputes, neither of you will want to back down. You may also be turned off by your Scorpio's complicated emotions.

Aquarius and **Sagittarius** enjoy each other's company. You also share a love of learning and both need as much intellectual freedom as you can get. This can be a very enduring relationship, whether it's platonic or passionate.

Aquarius and **Capricorn** will give you lots to think about because you'll be so busy trying to work out what makes each other tick. You may never arrive at an answer! You need to find some middle ground and to compromise.

Pisces

Pisces and **Pisces** is wonderful if you're both prepared to face facts rather than pretend your relationship is something it's not. Your life is likely to be highly romantic and you'll love creating a sophisticated home together.

Pisces and **Aries** will be very trying at times. It may also be painful, since your Arien is unlikely to understand how easily you're hurt. Even so, they will encourage you to grow another layer of skin and to laugh at yourself.

Pisces and **Taurus** is a very sensual combination. You'll bring out the romantic in one another, but there will be times when you'll wish your Taurean were less matter-of-fact, practical and sensible.

Pisces and **Gemini** can have fun together but it's awfully easy for you to feel hurt by your Gemini's glib turns of phrase. You may be happier as friends than lovers because your emotional needs are so different.

Pisces and **Cancer** is super because you both express love in the same way. It's wonderful being with someone who takes such care of you, although your Cancerian may not understand your need to be left alone sometimes.

Pisces and **Leo** find it hard to understand each other. At times you may find your Leo rather grand. You share a pronounced artistic streak and you're both very affectionate, but is that enough to keep you together?

Pisces and **Virgo** can be difficult for you. Your Virgo may trample all over your feelings in their well-meaning efforts to point out your faults and help you to rise above them. It all sounds like a lot of unnecessary criticism to you.

Pisces and **Libra** can be incredibly romantic. You could easily have a heady affair straight out of a Hollywood weepie, but staying together is another matter. You may drift apart because you're reluctant to face up to problems.

Pisces and **Scorpio** is a highly emotional and complex pairing. You're both very deep and sensitive, and it may take a while before you begin to understand each other. Once that happens, you won't look back.

Pisces and **Sagittarius** is dicey because you won't know what to make of your forthright Sagittarian. Why are they so blunt? Can't they see that it upsets you? You may be better as friends who share lots of exploits.

Pisces and **Capricorn** is fine if your Capricorn is happy to show their feelings. But if they're buttoned up or repressed, you won't know how to get through to them. Even so, you'll love the way they provide for you.

Pisces and **Aquarius** may as well be talking different languages for all the sense you make to each other. They enjoy talking about ideas that leave you baffled but will struggle to express their emotions in the way you need.

Aries

Aries and **Aries** is a very energetic combination, and you encourage each other in many different ways. Your relationship is competitive, sexy, exciting and sometimes pretty tempestuous!

Aries and **Taurus** can be difficult because you don't always understand each other. You love your Taurean's loyalty and affection but can feel frustrated if they're a great traditionalist or very stubborn.

Aries and **Gemini** get on like a house on fire and love hatching up new schemes together. But your differing sexual needs could cause problems, especially if your Gemini doesn't share your high sex drive.

Aries and **Cancer** is fine if your Cancerian will give you lots of personal freedom. However, they may be hurt if you aren't at home as much as they'd like, and they'll wonder what you're up to while you're away.

Aries and **Leo** really hit it off well and you'll have a lot of fun together. Sometimes you may wish your Leo would unbend a bit and be less dignified, but you adore the way they love and cherish you. It's great for your ego!

Aries and **Virgo** can be tricky because you have so little in common. You like to rush through life taking each day as it comes while they prefer to plan things in advance and then worry if they're doing the right thing. Irritating!

Aries and **Libra** have a lot to learn from each other. You enjoy the odd skirmish while your Libran prefers to keep the peace. Try to compromise over your differences rather than make them either/or situations.

Aries and **Scorpio** can be very dynamic and sexy together. Power is a huge aphrodisiac for you both so you're greatly attracted to each other. If you're a flirtatious Aries, your Scorpio will soon clip your wings.

Aries and **Sagittarius** are really excited by each other's company. You both adore challenges and will spur one another on to further feats and adventures. Your sex life is lively and interesting, and will keep you pretty busy.

Aries and **Capricorn** may not seem to have much in common on the surface. Yet you are both ambitious and will enjoy watching each other's progress. Sexually, things are surprisingly highly charged and naughty.

Aries and **Aquarius** have a lot of fun together but also share plenty of sparring matches. You get on better as friends than lovers because your Aquarian may not be nearly as interested in sex as you are.

Aries and **Pisces** is one of those tricky combinations that needs a lot of care if it's to succeed. It's horribly easy for you to upset your Piscean, often without realizing it, and you may get bored with having to reassure them so much.

Taurus

Taurus and **Taurus** is great because you're with someone who understands you inside out. Yet although this is comforting at first, it might start to become rather boring after a while, especially if you both like playing it safe.

Taurus and **Gemini** is good for keeping you on your toes, although you may find this tiring in the long term. They need a lot of change and variety, which can unsettle you and make you cling to stability and tradition.

Taurus and **Cancer** is lovely. You both appreciate the same sorts of things in life, such as good food, a loving partner and a cosy home. Once you get together you'll feel as though you've found your true soulmate.

Taurus and **Leo** share a love of luxury and the good things in life. You also know you can trust your Leo to be faithful and loyal, and in return you will shower them with plenty of admiration and moral support.

Taurus and **Virgo** is a very practical combination. Neither of you likes wasting time or money, although you may sometimes wish that your Virgo could be a little less austere and a bit more relaxed. But you still love them.

Taurus and **Libra** can have a very sensual and loving relationship. Neither of you likes conflict and you both need affectionate partners. But you may end up spending a lot of money together on all sorts of luxuries.

Taurus and **Scorpio** is a very powerful combination, especially in the bedroom. You both place a lot of importance on fidelity and loyalty, and you'll both believe that your relationship is the most important thing in your lives.

Taurus and **Sagittarius** don't really understand each other. You enjoy your home comforts and are generally content with life, while your Sagittarian always finds the grass is greener on the other side of the fence.

Taurus and **Capricorn** have a lot in common. You're both lusty, earthy and full of common sense. If you aren't careful, your relationship could get bogged down in practicalities, making you neglect the fun side of things.

Taurus and **Aquarius** struggle to appreciate each other. You enjoy sticking to the status quo whenever possible, while your Aquarian is always thinking of the future. You're both very stubborn, so rows can end in stalemate.

Taurus and **Pisces** is fine if your Piscean has their feet on the ground, because then you'll enjoy their sensitivity. But if they're very vague or other-worldly, you'll soon get annoyed and lose patience with them.

Taurus and **Aries** isn't the easiest combination for you. Although you enjoy your Arien's enthusiasm, it can wear a bit thin sometimes, especially when they're keen on something that you think is unrealistic or too costly.

Gemini

Gemini and **Gemini** can be great fun or one big headache. You both crave variety and busy lives, but if you're both very sociable you may rarely see each other. Your sex life may also fizzle out over time.

Gemini and **Cancer** is tricky if you're lovers rather than friends. Although you'll adore your Cancerian's displays of affection at first, after a while they may seem rather clingy or will make you feel trapped.

Gemini and **Leo** have lots of fun together. You genuinely like and love one another, although you may secretly be amused sometimes by your Leo's regal behaviour and want to give them some gentle teasing.

Gemini and **Virgo** hit it off surprisingly well. There's so much for you to talk about and plenty of scope for having a good laugh. You're tremendous friends, whether your relationship is sexual or purely platonic.

Gemini and **Libra** is one of the most enjoyable combinations of all for you. You can encourage your easy-going Libran to be more assertive while they help you to relax, and also bring out the romance in your soul.

Gemini and **Scorpio** make uncomfortable bedfellows but good friends. You have very little in common sexually but are intrigued by each other's minds. You share an insatiable curiosity about human nature.

Gemini and **Sagittarius** have a really good time together. You especially enjoy learning new things from one another and never run out of things to talk about. Travel and books are just two of your many shared enthusiasms.

Gemini and **Capricorn** isn't very easy because you're so different. At first you're intrigued by your Capricorn's responsibility and common sense, but after a while they may seem a little staid or stuffy for you.

Gemini and **Aquarius** are fantastic friends. You're used to having the upper hand intellectually with people but here is someone who makes you think and encourages you to look at life in a new way.

Gemini and **Pisces** can be tricky because it's easy to hurt your Piscean's feelings without even realizing it. Neither of you is very keen on facing up to harsh reality, which causes problems if you both avoid dealing with the facts.

Gemini and **Aries** is tremendous fun and you'll spend a lot of time laughing. If even half the plans you make come to fruition, you'll have a fantastic time together with never a dull moment.

Gemini and **Taurus** can make you wonder what you're doing wrong. Your Taurean may seem bemused or even slightly alarmed by you, and positively threatened by your need for as much variety in your life as possible.

Cancer

Cancer and **Cancer** is wonderful because you're able to take refuge in each other. You'll lavish a lot of time and effort on your home. Problems will arise if one of you doesn't get on well with the other one's family or friends.

Cancer and **Leo** share a love of family life, and you may even agree to give it priority over everything else. You'll be very proud of your Leo's achievements but will fret if these take them away from home too often.

Cancer and **Virgo** have a lot to teach each other. You'll learn from your Virgo how to do things methodically and carefully, and you'll encourage them to be more demonstrative and loving. It should work well!

Cancer and **Libra** is great if you have shared goals. You both understand the importance of ambition and will readily support one another. You enjoy being with someone who isn't afraid to show their affection.

Cancer and **Scorpio** is a very emotional and satisfying pairing. You know you can reveal your true feelings to your Scorpio, and you'll encourage them to do the same with you. Sexually, you'll really be in your element.

Cancer and **Sagittarius** find it hard to appreciate each other. You may even feel as though you come from different planets because you operate on a very emotional level while your Sagittarian prefers to stick to the facts.

Cancer and **Capricorn** is a case of opposites attracting. You both need what the other one can offer, and you'll be especially pleased if your Capricorn's capacity for hard work will provide a roof over your head and a stable home.

Cancer and **Aquarius** can be quirky friends but you'll struggle to sustain an emotional relationship because you're chalk and cheese. Your need for love and reassurance may be very difficult for your Aquarian to deal with.

Cancer and **Pisces** are really happy together. It's great knowing that you're with someone who understands your deep emotional needs and your complicated personality. You'll also revel in taking care of your Piscean.

Cancer and **Aries** can work if you both make allowances for each other. You need to give your Aries a lot of freedom because they'll get very angry if they feel they're tied to your apron strings.

Cancer and **Taurus** is a marriage made in heaven. You both need a happy, comfortable home and you also share a love of food. Your relationship may be so self-sufficient that you barely need anyone else in your lives.

Cancer and **Gemini** is OK if you don't spend too much time together! You'll feel slightly threatened by your Gemini's need for an active and independent social life, and they'll resent being expected to spend so much time at home.

Compatibility in Love and Sex at a glance

M \ F	♈	♉	♊	♋	♌	♍	♎	♏	♐	♑	♒	♓
♈	8	5	9	7	9	4	7	8	9	7	7	3
♉	6	8	4	10	7	8	8	7	3	8	2	8
♊	8	2	7	3	8	7	9	4	9	4	9	4
♋	5	10	4	8	6	5	6	8	2	9	2	8
♌	9	8	9	7	7	4	9	6	8	7	9	6
♍	4	8	6	4	4	7	6	7	7	9	4	4
♎	7	8	10	7	8	5	9	6	9	6	10	6
♏	7	9	4	7	6	6	7	10	5	6	5	7
♐	9	4	10	4	9	7	8	4	9	6	9	5
♑	7	8	4	9	6	8	6	4	4	8	4	5
♒	8	6	9	4	9	4	9	6	8	7	8	2
♓	7	6	7	9	6	7	6	9	7	5	4	9

1 = the pits
10 = the peaks

Key

♈ – Aries
♉ – Taurus
♊ – Gemini
♋ – Cancer
♌ – Leo
♍ – Virgo
♎ – Libra
♏ – Scorpio
♐ – Sagittarius
♑ – Capricorn
♒ – Aquarius
♓ – Pisces

Compatibility in Friendship at a glance

M \ F	♈	♉	♊	♋	♌	♍	♎	♏	♐	♑	♒	♓
♈	8	5	10	5	9	3	7	8	9	6	8	5
♉	6	9	6	10	7	8	7	6	4	9	3	9
♊	9	3	9	4	9	8	10	5	10	5	10	6
♋	6	9	4	9	5	4	6	9	4	10	3	9
♌	10	7	9	6	9	4	8	6	9	6	9	7
♍	5	9	8	4	4	8	5	8	8	10	5	6
♎	8	9	10	8	8	6	9	5	9	6	10	7
♏	7	8	5	8	7	7	6	9	4	5	6	8
♐	9	5	10	4	10	8	8	4	10	7	9	6
♑	6	9	5	10	6	9	5	5	4	9	5	6
♒	9	6	10	5	9	5	9	7	9	5	9	3
♓	6	7	6	10	6	8	7	9	8	6	4	10

1 = the pits
10 = the peaks

Key

♈ - Aries
♉ - Taurus
♊ - Gemini
♋ - Cancer
♌ - Leo
♍ - Virgo
♎ - Libra
♏ - Scorpio
♐ - Sagittarius
♑ - Capricorn
♒ - Aquarius
♓ - Pisces

YOUR ASTROLOGICAL HOLIDAY GUIDE

Have you ever wondered which holiday destination is right for your Sun sign, and what sort of activities you'll most enjoy when you get there? Well, your questions have been answered because this guide will give you some great ideas about how to have the holiday of a lifetime.

Leo

The one thing you crave above all else is sunshine, so it's very high up on your list of holiday priorities. You really come into your own when you're in a hot climate, although even you will wilt if the temperature rises too high. If you could have your heart's desire, you'd stay in a luxurious and exclusive resort on a tropical island, where you could do lots of celebrity-spotting while sipping cocktails on a palm-fringed beach. Too expensive? Then you would love going on safari and seeing your namesake lions prowling around, provided you didn't have to hammer in your own tent pegs every night. You do have your standards! Something else that would appeal is driving through a warm and friendly country in a chic or classic car, staying at delightful hotels along the way and buying lots of lovely clothes to wear when you get home.

Virgo

Although you may sound enthusiastic when your friends tell you about their trips to exotic locations, or describe meals containing the sort of wriggly items that you would squash to death if you found them in your garden, in reality you avoid them like the plague. Actually, you would probably rather have the plague than visit anywhere with dodgy hygiene, unsafe drinking water, poisonous creepy-crawlies, stomach-churning food or primitive plumbing. You're not the most adventurous traveller in the world and you don't care! Ideal holiday destinations for you include ski resorts where you can get exercise, hot chocolate and fresh air, or luxurious health farms that serve more than just a single lettuce leaf once a day. You would also adore a specialist holiday which caters for one of your interests and keeps your very clever brain fully occupied.

Libra

You can take any amount of luxury, relaxation and lotus-eating, especially when you're on holiday. You're too intelligent to be content spending a fortnight lying on a beach, but you might fancy visiting somewhere that offers the twin attractions of sparkling blue seas and plenty of culture. Decent food will also be high on your list of holiday essentials, because there's nothing you like better than working your way through a menu full of delicious temptations. You may even choose your destination or hotel purely on the strength of its cuisine or wine, and you'll do your best to sample as much of it as possible. If you're a typical Libran you have very sophisticated tastes and would enjoy visiting one of the great cities of the world, especially if you can combine sightseeing with an enjoyable tour of the best shops you can find.

Scorpio

You take such an intense approach to life that regular breaks are essential for you, because they help you to get things back in perspective. What's more, you're prepared to spend quite a lot of money on a holiday if necessary. If you can only take a short break, you adore the thought of staying in a fabulous country hotel, complete with spa, swimming pool, gardens and Michelin-starred dining room. So what if the bill makes your eyes water? You'll have had more than your money's worth in terms of enjoyment. You soon get bored if nothing is going on, so an activity holiday is perfect for you, especially if it offers plenty of excitement. You could learn to scuba-dive, brush up your skiing, go potholing or practise body-surfing. If you fancy something less daredevil, you might consider a wine-tasting holiday, a murder-mystery weekend or an Antarctic cruise.

Sagittarius

If you're a dyed-in-the-wool Sagittarian, you've probably already chosen the destinations of your next ten holidays. Travel is in your blood and you love exploring the world. You're unlikely to want to revisit the same place twice, although you might develop an abiding passion for a particular country and enjoy visiting different parts of it over the years. In the end, you'll be quite an expert on the subject. Your ideal holiday offers a combination of delicious food and drink, breathtaking scenery, comfortable sleeping arrangements, plenty of history, loads of culture and lots to look at. Grilling on a beach for two weeks, looking only at the sand, is your idea of hell. You'd much rather jump on a local bus and see where it takes you, laze the afternoon away in a restaurant or put your guidebook through its paces. You enjoy both heat and cold, which means you can be happy almost anywhere in the world.

Capricorn

You aren't entirely convinced by the need for holidays because they can seem like such an extravagance to you. Deep down, you'd probably rather stay at home and feel good about the money you've saved. If you are persuaded to go away, you won't want to throw your cash around willy-nilly and will choose somewhere that doesn't cost the earth. Nevertheless, you aren't keen on places that are too cheap and cheerful, and you're quite choosy about the company you keep. You might enjoy a skiing holiday, rock climbing or simply relaxing high in the mountains somewhere. You're very practical, so would also appreciate a holiday in which you learn a new skill or craft. You have a strong conservative streak, so will avoid anywhere that's too exotic, strange or dangerous. Instead, you'll choose places that feel familiar, and preferably where there's no language barrier.

Aquarius

The last thing you want to do on holiday is be surrounded by crowds and feel that you're part of a gigantic marketing machine. Instead, you're drawn to places that are off the beaten track, unfashionable (so you don't have to rub shoulders with every Tom, Dick and Harry) or are yet to be discovered by most people. You have no interest in simple beach holidays, unless you can alternate sunbathing with plenty of sightseeing. Destinations steeped in history and culture are ideal for you, because you love tuning in to the atmosphere and learning more about the country you're visiting. It's also essential that the place offers peace and quiet, so you can read all those books you've brought with you. For you, part of the pleasure of going on holiday is meeting the locals, so it's important that you visit somewhere friendly and welcoming.

Pisces

You're so sensitive to atmospheres that you need to choose your holiday destination very carefully. Try to avoid political trouble spots or places that are heaving with fellow holidaymakers because your delicate nerves will soon become jangled and you'll start longing to go home again. You adore being near water, whether it's a lake or an ocean, and find it very relaxing just to listen to the sound of the waves while gazing into space. The clear blue waters of a tropical island would be paradise for you, because you love swimming. You aren't comfortable if you have to rough it, so are happiest staying somewhere that offers plenty of luxury. However, you'll be very disturbed if there's a marked contrast between your level of comfort and that of the local people. Your ideal holiday includes plenty of sightseeing, because you love soaking up the atmosphere and getting a strong sense of the spirit of the place.

Aries

In an ideal world, you would never visit the same holiday destination twice because you hate that sense of 'been there, done that'. Besides, there's a whole world out there waiting to be explored, so why waste your valuable holiday time going back to the same old resort year after year? If you're a typical Arien, excitement, heat and plenty of action are the ingredients for a perfect holiday. If a little courage is required, then so much the better. You'll enjoy regaling your friends and family with eye-popping tales of your bravery as you mastered white-water rafting, braved huge rollers on your surfboard, went on safari, trekked through a jungle or endured the baking heat of a desert. If you have to choose something that you consider to be more tame, you'll enjoy a fly-drive or activity holiday. At a pinch, you might be persuaded to lie on a beach but you won't want to do it for long because you'll soon get bored.

Taurus

As the great hedonist of the zodiac, your idea of a blissful holiday is one in which you do as little as possible while other people attend to your every whim. If money is no object you'll be in seventh heaven staying in a luxury hotel that serves delectable drinks, sumptuous food and has the finest cotton sheets. Some signs are completely incapable of sitting around doing nothing but you could turn it into an art form, given half a chance. If you have to lower your holiday sights through a lack of cash, you'd enjoy staying in a self-catering cottage in beautiful surroundings. The cottage must have all mod cons, of course, because the charm of pumping your own water from a tumbledown well would pall after the first ten minutes. You feel revived and rejuvenated when you're surrounded by nature and beauty, so you might enjoy a holiday tour of famous gardens, a visit to a country renowned for its autumn colours or a trip to an unspoilt island paradise.

Gemini

Variety is the spice of life for you, so you won't want to visit the same destination year after year. Instead, you like the thought of trying somewhere completely different each time, because half the fun is reading about it before you go and then trying to cram a selection of indispensable travel guides and phrase books into your already bulging suitcase. You need to keep on the move, too, so are happiest if the local transport is excellent or you can hire a car to get around. You're thrilled by bustling cities, especially if you can sit in a café and watch the world go by, then shop to your heart's content. Destinations that are steeped in history or culture also appeal to you. Another option is to take an activity holiday in which you'll learn something new; it could be anything from watercolour painting to belly-dancing.

Cancer

Familiarity breeds content for you, so you can feel uneasy when visiting somewhere for the first time. What if you don't like it? You're the sort of person who is welcomed with open arms by hoteliers because if you like the place you'll return year after year, and you'll take your nearest and dearest with you. It's a rare Cancerian who doesn't enjoy eating, so you'll want to choose a destination in which the food is to your liking, and you'll hope that there's lots of it. You can't cope with anything too exotic or strange, and you need to take care of your sensitive tummy, which rules out some of the more far-flung corners of the world. You also can't tolerate extreme heat or humidity. You love being near water and would enjoy a relaxing beach holiday or staying at a hotel on a large lake. Another option is a self-catering holiday in which you can create a home from home.

BORN ON THE CUSP?

Were you born on the cusp of Leo – at the beginning or end of the sign? If so, you may have spent years wondering which sign you belong to. Are you a Leo, a Cancerian or a Virgo? Different horoscope books and columns can give different dates for when the Sun moves into each sign, leaving you utterly confused. Yet none of these dates is wrong, as you'll discover in a minute. Checking your birth date, and time if you know it, in the list given in this chapter will allow you to solve the mystery at long last!

Many people believe that the Sun moves like clockwork from one sign to another on a specific day each year. But this isn't always true. For instance, let's look at the dates for the sign of Leo. On the cover of this book I give them as 23 July to 23 August. Very often, the Sun will obediently change signs on these days but sometimes it won't. It can move from Cancer into Leo on 22 or 23 July and it can move into Virgo on 22, 23 or 24 August.

So how can you find out which sign you belong to if you were born on the cusp of Leo? The only information you need is the place, year, day and the time of your birth if you know it. It helps to have the time of birth because if the Sun did move signs on your birthday, you can see whether it moved before or after you were born. If you don't have an exact time, even knowing whether it was morning or afternoon can be a help. For instance, if you were born in the morning and the Sun didn't move signs on your birthday until the afternoon, that will be enough information to tell you which sign is yours.

You need to know the place in case you were born outside the United Kingdom and have to convert its local time zone to British time. This information is easily available in many diaries and reference books.

Four Simple Steps to Find your Sun Sign

1 Write down the year, day, time and place of your birth, in that order.

2 If you were born outside the United Kingdom, you must convert your birth date and time to British time by adding or subtracting the relevant number of hours from it. This may take your birthday into the following day or back to the previous day. If so, write down this new date and time because that will be the one you use in the following calculations. If summer time was operating you must deduct the relevant number of hours to convert your birth time to Greenwich Mean Time (GMT).

3 If you were born in Britain, look up your year of birth in the list of British Summer Time (BST) changes to see if BST was operating when you were born. If it was, subtract the appropriate number of hours from your birth time to convert it to GMT. This may give you a different time and/or date of birth.

4 Look up your year of birth in the Annual Sun Sign Changes list. If you were born within these dates and times, you are a Leo. If you were born outside them, you are either a Cancerian if you were born in July, or a Virgo if you were born in August.

Two Examples

Here are a couple of examples so you can see how the process works. Let's say we're looking for the Sun sign of Chris, who was born in the UK on 23 July 1942 at 01:30. Start by checking the list of British Summer Time dates to see if BST was operating at the time of her birth. It was, but you will see that she was born during a phase when two hours had been added, so you have to subtract two hours from her birth time to convert it to GMT. This gives her a birth time of 23:30 on the previous day – therefore, her GMT birthday is 22 July and her GMT birth time is 23:30. Write this down, so you don't forget it. Now turn to the Annual Sun Sign Changes list and look for 1942, her year of birth. In that year, the Sun moved into Leo on 23 July at 12:08, and Chris's GMT birth time was at 23:30 the previous day, so she is a Cancerian, not a Leo. However, if she had been born on 23 July 1942 at 15:30 (which gives her a GMT birth time of 13:30 on the same day), the Sun would have been in Leo so she would be a Leo.

But what would her sign be if she were born on 23 August 1952 at 06:30? First check the dates in the BST list for 1952 (note the year change from the above example). You will see she was born during a period when one hour had been added for BST, so you must subtract one hour to convert her birth time to GMT. This changes it to 05:30 on 23 August 1952. Write this down. Now look up the Sun sign dates for 1952. Look at the August date. The Sun was in Leo until 23 August at 05:02. So Chris's GMT birth time was after the Sun had moved into Virgo, making her a Virgo.

Dates for British Summer Time

If your birthday falls within these dates and times, you were born during BST and will have to convert your birth time back to GMT. To do this, subtract one hour from your birth time. If you were born during a period that is marked *, you must subtract two hours from your birth time to convert it to GMT. All times are given in BST, using the 24-hour clock.

1920 28 Mar, 02:00–25 Oct, 01:59 inc
1921 3 Apr, 02:00–3 Oct, 01:59 inc
1922 26 Mar, 02:00–8 Oct, 01:59 inc
1923 22 Apr, 02:00–16 Sep, 01:59 inc
1924 13 Apr, 02:00–21 Sep, 01:59 inc
1925 19 Apr, 02:00–4 Oct, 01:59 inc
1926 18 Apr, 02:00–3 Oct, 01:59 inc
1927 10 Apr, 02:00–2 Oct, 01:59 inc
1928 22 Apr, 02:00–7 Oct, 01:59 inc
1929 21 Apr, 02:00–6 Oct, 01:59 inc
1930 13 Apr, 02:00–5 Oct, 01:59 inc
1931 19 Apr, 02:00–4 Oct, 01:59 inc
1932 17 Apr, 02:00–2 Oct, 01:59 inc
1933 9 Apr, 02:00–8 Oct, 01:59 inc
1934 22 Apr, 02:00–7 Oct, 01:59 inc
1935 14 Apr, 02:00–6 Oct, 01:59 inc
1936 19 Apr, 02:00–4 Oct, 01:59 inc
1937 18 Apr, 02:00–3 Oct, 01:59 inc
1938 10 Apr, 02:00–2 Oct, 01:59 inc
1939 16 Apr, 02:00–19 Nov, 01:59 inc
1940 25 Feb, 02:00–31 Dec, 23:59 inc
1941 1 Jan, 00:00–4 May, 01:59 inc
1941 4 May, 02:00–10 Aug, 01:59 inc*
1941 10 Aug, 02:00–31 Dec, 23:59 inc
1942 1 Jan, 00:00–5 Apr, 01:59 inc
1942 5 Apr, 02:00–9 Aug, 01:59 inc*
1942 9 Aug, 02:00–31 Dec, 23:59 inc
1943 1 Jan, 00:00–4 Apr, 01:59 inc
1943 4 Apr, 02:00–15 Aug, 01:59 inc*
1943 15 Aug, 02:00–31 Dec, 23:59 inc
1944 1 Jan, 00:00–2 Apr, 01:59 inc
1944 2 Apr, 02:00–17 Sep, 01:59 inc*
1944 17 Sep, 02:00–31 Dec, 23:59 inc
1945 1 Jan, 02:00–2 Apr, 01:59 inc
1945 2 Apr, 02:00–15 Jul, 01:59 inc*
1945 15 Jul, 02:00–7 Oct, 01:59 inc
1946 14 Apr, 02:00–6 Oct, 01:59 inc
1947 16 Mar, 02:00–13 Apr, 01:59 inc
1947 13 Apr, 02:00–10 Aug, 01:59 inc*
1947 10 Aug, 02:00–2 Nov, 01:59 inc
1948 14 Mar, 02:00–31 Oct, 01:59 inc
1949 3 Apr, 02:00–30 Oct, 01:59 inc
1950 16 Apr, 02:00–22 Oct, 01:59 inc
1951 15 Apr, 02:00–21 Oct, 01:59 inc
1952 20 Apr, 02:00–26 Oct, 01:59 inc
1953 19 Apr, 02:00–4 Oct, 01:59 inc
1954 11 Apr, 02:00–3 Oct, 01:59 inc
1955 17 Apr, 02:00–2 Oct, 01:59 inc
1956 22 Apr, 02:00–7 Oct, 01:59 inc
1957 14 Apr, 02:00–6 Oct, 01:59 inc
1958 20 Apr, 02:00–5 Oct, 01:59 inc
1959 19 Apr, 02:00–4 Oct, 01:59 inc
1960 10 Apr, 02:00–2 Oct, 01:59 inc
1961 26 Mar, 02:00–29 Oct, 01:59 inc
1962 25 Mar, 02:00–28 Oct, 01:59 inc
1963 31 Mar, 02:00–27 Oct, 01:59 inc
1964 22 Mar, 02:00–25 Oct, 01:59 inc
1965 21 Mar, 02:00–24 Oct, 01:59 inc
1966 20 Mar, 02:00–23 Oct, 01:59 inc
1967 19 Mar, 02:00–29 Oct, 01:59 inc
1968 18 Feb, 02:00–31 Dec, 23:59 inc
1969 1 Jan, 00:00–31 Dec, 23:59 inc
1970 1 Jan, 00:00–31 Dec, 23:59 inc
1971 1 Jan, 00:00–31 Oct, 01:59 inc
1972 19 Mar, 02:00–29 Oct, 01:59 inc
1973 18 Mar, 02:00–28 Oct, 01:59 inc
1974 17 Mar, 02:00–27 Oct, 01:59 inc
1975 16 Mar, 02:00–26 Oct, 01:59 inc
1976 21 Mar, 02:00–24 Oct, 01:59 inc
1977 20 Mar, 02:00–23 Oct, 01:59 inc
1978 19 Mar, 02:00–29 Oct, 01:59 inc
1979 18 Mar, 02:00–28 Oct, 01:59 inc
1980 16 Mar, 02:00–26 Oct, 01:59 inc
1981 29 Mar, 01:00–25 Oct, 00:59 inc
1982 28 Mar, 01:00–24 Oct, 00:59 inc
1983 27 Mar, 01:00–23 Oct, 00:59 inc
1984 25 Mar, 01:00–28 Oct, 00:59 inc
1985 31 Mar, 01:00–27 Oct, 00:59 inc
1986 30 Mar, 01:00–26 Oct, 00:59 inc
1987 29 Mar, 01:00–25 Oct, 00:59 inc
1988 27 Mar, 01:00–23 Oct, 00:59 inc
1989 26 Mar, 01:00–29 Oct, 00:59 inc

1990 25 Mar, 01:00–28 Oct, 00:59 inc
1991 31 Mar, 01:00–27 Oct, 00:59 inc
1992 29 Mar, 01:00–25 Oct, 00:59 inc
1993 28 Mar, 01:00–24 Oct, 00:59 inc
1994 27 Mar, 01:00–23 Oct, 00:59 inc
1995 26 Mar, 01:00–22 Oct, 00:59 inc
1996 31 Mar, 01:00–27 Oct, 00:59 inc
1997 30 Mar, 01:00–26 Oct, 00:59 inc
1998 29 Mar, 01:00–25 Oct, 00:59 inc
1999 28 Mar, 01:00–31 Oct, 00:59 inc
2000 26 Mar, 01:00–29 Oct, 00:59 inc
2001 25 Mar, 01:00–28 Oct, 00:59 inc
2002 31 Mar, 01:00–27 Oct, 00:59 inc
2003 30 Mar, 01:00–26 Oct, 00:59 inc
2004 28 Mar, 01:00–31 Oct, 00:59 inc

* Subtract two hours from the birth time to convert it to GMT.

Annual Sun Sign Changes

If your birthday falls within these dates and times, you are a Leo. If you were born in July before the first date and time, you are a Cancerian. If you were born in August after the second date and time, you are a Virgo. All times are given in GMT, using the 24-hour clock.

1920 23 Jul, 04:35–23 Aug, 11:21 inc
1921 23 Jul, 10:31–23 Aug, 17:15 inc
1922 23 Jul, 16:20–23 Aug, 23:04 inc
1923 23 Jul, 22:01–24 Aug, 04:51 inc
1924 23 Jul, 03:58–23 Aug, 10:47 inc
1925 23 Jul, 09:45–23 Aug, 16:33 inc
1926 23 Jul, 15:25–23 Aug, 22:13 inc
1927 23 Jul, 21:17–24 Aug, 04:05 inc
1928 23 Jul, 03:03–23 Aug, 09:53 inc
1929 23 Jul, 08:54–23 Aug, 15:41 inc
1930 23 Jul, 14:42–23 Aug, 21:26 inc
1931 23 Jul, 20:22–24 Aug, 03:10 inc
1932 23 Jul, 02:18–23 Aug, 09:06 inc
1933 23 Jul, 08:06–23 Aug, 14:52 inc
1934 23 Jul, 13:43–23 Aug, 20:31 inc
1935 23 Jul, 19:33–24 Aug, 02:23 inc
1936 23 Jul, 01:18–23 Aug, 08:10 inc
1937 23 Jul, 07:07–23 Aug, 13:57 inc
1938 23 Jul, 12:58–23 Aug, 19:45 inc
1939 23 Jul, 18:37–24 Aug, 01:31 inc
1940 23 Jul, 00:35–23 Aug, 07:28 inc
1941 23 Jul, 06:27–23 Aug, 13:16 inc
1942 23 Jul, 12:08–23 Aug, 18:58 inc
1943 23 Jul, 18:05–24 Aug, 00:54 inc
1944 22 Jul, 23:56–23 Aug, 06:46 inc
1945 23 Jul, 05:46–23 Aug, 12:35 inc
1946 23 Jul, 11:38–23 Aug, 18:26 inc
1947 23 Jul, 17:15–24 Aug, 00:08 inc
1948 22 Jul, 23:08–23 Aug, 06:02 inc
1949 23 Jul, 04:57–23 Aug, 11:48 inc
1950 23 Jul, 10:30–23 Aug, 17:23 inc
1951 23 Jul, 16:21–23 Aug, 23:16 inc
1952 22 Jul, 22:08–23 Aug, 05:02 inc
1953 23 Jul, 03:53–23 Aug, 10:45 inc
1954 23 Jul, 09:45–23 Aug, 16:35 inc
1955 23 Jul, 15:25–23 Aug, 22:18 inc
1956 22 Jul, 21:20–23 Aug, 04:14 inc
1957 23 Jul, 03:15–23 Aug, 10:07 inc
1958 23 Jul, 08:51–23 Aug, 15:45 inc
1959 23 Jul, 14:46–23 Aug, 21:43 inc
1960 22 Jul, 20:38–23 Aug, 03:34 inc
1961 23 Jul, 02:24–23 Aug, 09:18 inc
1962 23 Jul, 08:19–23 Aug, 15:12 inc
1963 23 Jul, 14:00–23 Aug, 20:57 inc
1964 22 Jul, 19:53–23 Aug, 02:51 inc
1965 23 Jul, 01:49–23 Aug, 08:42 inc
1966 23 Jul, 07:24–23 Aug, 14:17 inc
1967 23 Jul, 13:16–23 Aug, 20:12 inc
1968 22 Jul, 19:08–23 Aug, 02:03 inc
1969 23 Jul, 00:49–23 Aug, 07:43 inc

1970 23 Jul, 06:38–23 Aug, 13:34 inc
1971 23 Jul, 12:15–23 Aug, 19:15 inc
1972 22 Jul, 18:03–23 Aug, 01:03 inc
1973 22 Jul, 23:56–23 Aug, 06:53 inc
1974 23 Jul, 05:31–23 Aug, 12:28 inc
1975 23 Jul, 11:23–23 Aug, 18:23 inc
1976 22 Jul, 17:19–23 Aug, 00:18 inc
1977 22 Jul, 23:04–23 Aug, 06:00 inc
1978 23 Jul, 05:01–23 Aug, 11:57 inc
1979 23 Jul, 10:49–23 Aug, 17:47 inc
1980 22 Jul, 16:43–22 Aug, 23:41 inc
1981 22 Jul, 22:41–23 Aug, 05:38 inc
1982 23 Jul, 04:16–23 Aug, 11:15 inc
1983 23 Jul, 10:05–23 Aug, 17:07 inc
1984 22 Jul, 15:59–22 Aug, 23:00 inc
1985 22 Jul, 21:37–23 Aug, 04:36 inc
1986 23 Jul, 03:25–23 Aug, 10:26 inc
1987 23 Jul, 09:07–23 Aug, 16:10 inc
1988 22 Jul, 14:52–22 Aug, 21:54 inc
1989 22 Jul, 20:46–23 Aug, 03:46 inc
1990 23 Jul, 02:22–23 Aug, 09:21 inc
1991 23 Jul, 08:12–23 Aug, 15:13 inc
1992 22 Jul, 14:10–22 Aug, 21:10 inc
1993 22 Jul, 19:52–23 Aug, 02:50 inc
1994 23 Jul, 01:42–23 Aug, 08:44 inc
1995 23 Jul, 07:31–23 Aug, 14:35 inc
1996 22 Jul, 13:20–22 Aug, 20:23 inc
1997 22 Jul, 19:16–23 Aug, 02:19 inc
1998 23 Jul, 00:56–23 Aug, 08:59 inc
1999 23 Jul, 06:45–23 Aug, 13:51 inc
2000 22 Jul, 12:44–22 Aug, 19:49 inc
2001 22 Jul, 18:27–23 Aug, 01:27 inc
2002 23 Jul, 00:16–23 Aug, 07:17 inc
2003 23 Jul, 06:05–23 Aug, 13:08 inc
2004 22 Jul, 11:51–22 Aug, 18:53 inc